SECULAR EDUCATION
AND THE LOGIC OF RELIGION

SECULAR EDUCATION
AND THE
LOGIC OF RELIGION

Heslington Lectures, University of York, 1966

by

NINIAN SMART

*Professor of Religious Studies
in the University of Lancaster*

FABER AND FABER

24 Russell Square

London

First published in 1968
by Faber and Faber Limited
24 Russell Square London WC1
Printed in Great Britain by
Latimer Trend & Co Ltd Plymouth
All rights reserved

S.B.N. 571 08284 9

© *Ninian Smart 1968*

CONTENTS

INTRODUCTION

I am here concerned with the logic of religious education and with the consequences of that logic in a secular or religiously neutralist society such as ours in Britain. I am not here much concerned with the important question of *how* religion should be taught in schools, colleges and universities. I am concerned with the *content* of what should be taught.

I begin from a consideration of the place and nature of theology, and so I begin from the standpoint of higher education. But what is said here applies by implication to school curricula. In the last chapter I refer to this aspect of the matter. Since what I say has to do with the logic of the subject, together with the requirements of an open or secular society, the conclusions should apply throughout a secular educational system. It is a quite different question as to how and when the different elements of the subject should be introduced. When and how young people can grasp certain concepts and the like is a problem relevant to educational technology. But we should first have a clear idea of what the aims of this technology should be.

There is no intention here to argue for secular theology in that other sense of *secular* which has to do with the secular city and the secular meaning of the gospel. I have no special liking for these formulations of the Christian faith : in their application to non-Western cultures they seem to me to be simply neo-colonialist. The suggestion is that with the spread of technology, Indians will end up like us. Having lost the Raj, we no doubt want the future. No, I am rather here concerned with our situation in a secular society in the sense of an open, religiously neutralist one—where men can make up their own minds about religious and ideological matters.

7

But it is not possible to say anything sensible about the logic of religious studies without giving examples. Hence the middle three chapters are in fact constituted by arguments on different themes—one within the area of doctrine and philosophical theology; one within the area of New Testament history; and one within the area of the comparative study of religion. In the last chapter the lessons are applied. It is to be hoped that the reader will enjoy these three arguments in their own right, independently of any special and ultimate application to educational problems.

This book has arisen out of the Heslington Lectures given under the title 'The Nature of Theology and the Idea of a Secular University' which I delivered in the University of York in 1966. I am deeply grateful for the honour and enjoyment this invitation gave me, and to those kind people who entertained me so excellently. I am grateful too to Lord James for his encouragement over publishing the book (which I had not originally intended to do) and to the Reverend Daniel Jenkins of the University of Sussex for his help in this matter and for his comments. Likewise I have benefited from the comments and criticisms of Mr. Alan Pringle. My colleague Dr. Neville Birdsall has helpfully discussed the thesis about Barabbas argued in the third chapter, and has been a source of encouragement to me in a field with which I am all too unfamiliar.

The last chapter has been recast, to be relevant to a wider audience than the original one, but otherwise the substance of the lectures is reproduced.

NINIAN SMART
Edgbaston, July 1967

CHAPTER I

IF NOT THE QUEEN, THEN WHAT?

Theology was once looked upon as the queen of the sciences: now it is often regarded as the knave of arts. Its position is doubtful for at least two reasons.

First, ours is a pluralistic society, and a great number of those involved in education are sceptical of the truth of Christianity. If theology is supposed to be Christian, then its basis is not acknowledged by a great number of teachers and students. Second, even if theology may protect itself from such scepticism by claiming merely to be concerned with linguistic and historical questions about the Bible and so forth, thus becoming as 'objective' and scientific as other linguistic and historical disciplines, there remains the suspicion that the choice of documents for deep investigation—the Bible and early Christian texts—presupposes a view about revelation which the sceptics cannot share. The presence of departments or faculties of theology in modern universities can thus seem unwarrantable. It can even seem sinister—a sign of the covert continued power of some religious establishment in a secular context.

Alas, questions about religious studies are rarely treated with enough dispassion. Prejudices bristle, misconceptions abound and interests are quietly promoted. At the same time, there can be no doubt that the place of religion in our educational system is an important issue.

Although much that I shall have to say is more directly relevant to theology in the universities, it will in essence also be relevant to religious studies in colleges of education and in schools. There is an organic connection between the teaching and study of religion in all forms and stages of education. Consequently, part of the aim of these lectures is to make some practical suggestions about the content of teaching and research in this area.

But it will be necessary to precede this 'practical' side with a theoretical inquiry. For what theology is cannot be properly understood except in the context of certain theoretical considerations deriving from the nature of religion and religious belief. We first have to understand the inner logic of religious studies before we can draw conclusions about what their content should be in practice.

Theology, whether seen as queen, knave or plain card, is an enigmatic figure. It engages in a great number of diverse and sometimes strange occupations. Its practitioners are liable to wrestle with Greek, Hebrew, Syriac, Coptic; to compare manuscript traditions; to write history; to philosophize; to systematize; to study worship; to contemplate problems in ethics. How can we grasp its true nature?

First, let us note a significant omission in the very title 'theology'. It is assumed, but not always explicitly stated, that theology is Christian theology. Yet of course there are other theologies—Muslim, Hindu and so on. If we hesitate to use the phrase 'Buddhist theology' it is only because Buddhism does not entail belief in God, and thus the word 'theology' is inappropriate. At any rate, there are Buddhist doctrines. If we want a general term to cover such a case (and indeed to cover the case of a quasi-religion, Marxism), perhaps 'doctrinal inquiry' is useful.

Thus we can say that there are many types of doctrinal inquiry, Christian theology being only one of them. Nevertheless, I shall for the moment confine attention to theology in the Christian sense, though I am deeply committed to the importance of a wider consideration of doctrinal inquiries in our schools and universities.

But the fact that we make a certain assumption in speaking of theology *tout court* is not without significance. It draws attention to the great assumption already contained in the word: that there is a God. Giving an exposition of Newman, Mr. John Coulson writes:

> Throughout his history man has concerned himself with the problem of a supreme Being—God. A body of knowledge has grown up, to which we give the name of theology, and any curriculum of liberal knowledge, or university professing to take all knowledge for its province, denies the significance of such an existing body of knowledge at its own risk. This, as far as the university is concerned, is what Newman means by theology: 'the science of God, or the truths we know about God put into a system'.*

Many will find that these words grate upon their ears and intellects.

Since 'I know that P' implies the truth of P, and since 'I know so-and-so' implies the existence of so-and-so, those who are sceptical about God's existence will not be able to speak of *knowledge* about or of God. For the sceptic the very word 'theology' covers a great God-shaped blank. The above quotation, too, gives theology a quite spurious air of consolidated success and empirical assurance. It represents to us that man has gradually built up a whole nexus of facts about God, through long concern with the subject. This is false, for two reasons.

First, as we have already mentioned, Buddhism does not involve belief in a Creator. Far from it: Theravada Buddhism in effect rejects the belief; and even if there are some echoes of theism in Mahayana Buddhism the result is very different from that faith in a Creator expressed in the Judaeo-Christian tradition. Buddhism—a fabulously successful missionary religion—belies the assumption that men have tended everywhere to concern themselves with a Supreme Being or God. Of course, it was natural for Newman to think that men have always been oriented towards a concern for God or at least the

* John Coulson (ed.), *Theology and the University*, London, 1964, pp. 51–2.

11

gods. He belonged to the era before a real understanding of Eastern cultures was widely available to the West, and he thus moved within the ambit of typical European cultural tribalism.

Second, the idea that men have gradually built up a science (as it were) of God is spurious, because even arguing from the assumption that there is a God as described in Christian faith, we must soon be aware of the degree to which men have disputed about his nature. What we have rather is a certain growing and bifurcating tradition in Christendom. The cumulative reflection upon revelation, Christian origins and the pattern of the universe is not rightly called a science even in that peculiar sense of the term used by Newman, namely truths put into a system. The different branches of Christianity have somewhat different systems; individuals within and without these branches have varying systems. Not everyone can be absolutely right. In view of the debatable and plural character of theology in this sense it is unsatisfactory to regard it, question-beggingly, as a system of truths.

We must note then that the term usually makes two big assumptions: first, that there is a God, and second that it is the Christian tradition with which it is essentially concerned.

Now it might be replied to this that there is a sense of the term which at least does not make the first assumption. Can we not simply study Christian texts, Christian history and so forth from an objective, scientific point of view? Such a study yields results independently of any faith in the truth of the Bible as a record of God's self-revelation. Is this not the proper sense in which we speak of theology in the secular university?

The objection is well taken, for it points to the fundamental ambiguity in the knave of arts. The fundamental ambiguity is that one can approach religious studies in two quite different ways. We can consider religious phenomena and beliefs from a purely historical and descriptive point of view on the one hand; and we can approach them as relevant to, or as enshrining, claims about the nature of reality. We can, that is, treat religion historically or doctrinally. This is so, whether our standpoint be religious or atheistic. The atheist who argues for the falsity of belief in God is going beyond a simply descriptive account of religion. Likewise the Christian who preaches, or who engages in apologetics, is doing more than making historical and descriptive remarks about Christianity.

I have used the terms 'historical' and 'doctrinal' to point to the contrast between the two approaches. But the latter expression is not altogether a good one for the purpose. Although a religion such as Christianity teaches certain doctrines, doctrines are by no means everything. The Christian faith has prescriptions about conduct, a right mode of worship (or modes thereof), an institutional vehicle, the Church, and so on. As we shall see, a religion is a multi-dimensional thing, and the doctrinal side represents only one dimension.

One needs then a wider word. It is required to cover cases of commending the faith, of arguing for its truth, of endorsing religious values, etc., and cases of doing the reverse (as when one may criticize a faith as untrue, or dangerous, or decadent, or pernicious, or nonsensical, etc.). In all these cases one is not disputing that John XXIII was a Pope or that Christianity is nearly two thousand years old or that there are many Christians in Italy. One is rather taking some stand about or arguing about the validity or value of a faith or of some aspect thereof. The distinction between making a religious claim and asserting something descriptive about religion is used in the joke about the man who asked another 'Do you believe in baptism?' 'Believe in it?' the other man answered: 'I've seen it done.'

If in a broad sense we can say that descriptive studies are historical (even if they are sometimes about contemporary events or transcultural analogies and so on), then it may be useful to employ the term *parahistorical* to refer to those studies and arguments which concern the truth, value, etc., of religion.

The question of whether Jesus lived in Galilee is, on this usage, an historical question; but the question of whether he died for men's sins is parahistorical (but note that the question of whether he thought he died for men's sins reverts to the

13

historical side). The question of whether mystical experience contains an unvarying central core is an historical question; but the question of whether one knows God through mystical experience is a parahistorical one. The problem of the degree to which a particular religion is sociologically determined is an historical problem (on this usage); the question of whether its moral teachings are right is a parahistorical question.

It is of fundamental importance to bear this distinction in mind. The very notion of religious studies takes on a very different meaning according as we include in them, or fail to include in them, parahistorical questions. I shall argue later that they need to be included, because of the logic of the subject: but I shall also argue that this can only rightly be done by liberating theology from the narrow confines of its past.

Now whether or not we think that parahistorical approaches to religion are a proper component of formal education—they are, of course, entrenched in school education by virtue of the 1944 Education Act—they obviously are important. They belong to the general problem of deciding about the truth of ideologies. Whether, for instance, we are committed to a political liberalism which makes Humanist assumptions, or to Marxism, or to Christian Democracy in the European sense, our commitment will make some difference to the tangled ongoings of history. It will make some difference to our personal and professional conduct. It will in some degree influence our emotional reactions to the world into which we have been pitched. One cannot for these reasons divorce ideological from religious issues. Consequently, the parahistorical questions about religion are part of the general problem of ideology—or if you like, metaphysics.

It is thus useful if we can come to any insight on how we might settle parahistorical problems. How would one, for instance, uncover the criteria of truth in religion? How would one set about answering questions about the truth of Christianity? These issues are relevant to the problem of how parahistorical approaches to religion can be sanely and sensitively incorporated

14

into religious studies. The issues are in effect part of the methodology of theology. Often a theological system will incorporate remarks about how we arrive at the truth—this complicates the matter. But it is a reason for saying that not only must one become involved in philosophizing about religion (discussing, for instance, the criteria of truth in general), but also in considering serious theological positions themselves.

However, it would be facile to think of religious ideas as existing just in people's heads or on paper. They can only be properly understood in their living milieu. Thus Christian theology has to be seen in its institutional and sacramental environment. It has to do with faith, with people, with worship. It is not *just* a piece of metaphysics, and not a free-floating ideology.

I have, of course, earlier remarked that there are divergences within the Christian tradition. It is somewhat oversimplifying matters to speak of 'Christian theology' *tout court*. But so as not to overload and complicate unduly the subsequent argument I shall consider a kind of ecumenical Christianity. I shall discuss the doctrine of Creation, for instance, in the next chapter: but I hope that the remarks I make do not exclude what would be demanded by way of belief in any of the major branches of contemporary Christendom.

In claiming that a theology or doctrinal inquiry is not just a free-floating affair, I am attempting to put proper weight on the fact that religious ideas are not just ideas but *religious* ideas. One can see this point more clearly by observing the nature of religion, which is a complex object—a six-dimensional one, as I shall argue.

One dimension of religion can be epitomized in what we have already started to discuss: namely the fact that religions typically teach *doctrines*. In Christianity, there is, for instance, the Trinity Doctrine, the doctrine of Creation and so on. In Buddhism, there is the *dharma*, summed up in such formulae as the Four Noble Truths. It is true that many ethnic religions in technologically primitive and pre-literate cultures do not for-

15

mally enunciate teachings about the nature of God, the world man, etc. They tend to spell out religion in myths. But it is typical of the major religions of the world—in the Indian, Semitic and Chinese cultures—to teach doctrines. It is therefore useful to speak of the *doctrinal dimension* of religion.

Secondly, a religion typically contains beliefs which are cast in story form, whether the stories concern actual historical events interpreted religiously or non-historical 'transcendental' or sacred events. Such stories of the gods, of God, of God's activities in history, of the career of the sacred teacher—these can, by a generous extension of the term, be called myths. I am in using this last word not intending any judgment about truth or falsity : I am not using the word in that everyday sense where 'myth' just means a false belief or what have you. On my usage, the Exodus, the stories of deliberations on Olympus, the Buddha's career, the accounts of the gods in the Pali canon— these belong to the *mythological dimension* of religion. Sometimes, we may note, it is not easy to draw a line between doctrine and myth. Sometimes the doctrine, indeed, results from reflection on and refinement of what is initially cast in mythological form : thus between *Genesis* and Aquinas' theology of Creation there is a transition of this sort.

Thirdly, a religion prescribes an ethical path. Its ethics are often woven in part out of doctrinal and mythological threads. Jesus' death on the Cross illuminates the meaning of Christian love, for example. We may call this the *ethical dimension* of religion.

These three dimensions can be said to represent the teachings of a religion : they sum up its *Weltanschauung* : they express the perspective in which the adherent views the world and himself. But even if we have gone beyond the notion that the world-view of a religion is simply expressed in doctrinal propositions, for it is clothed too in myth, symbolism, ethical prescriptions, we must go further and see the relation between these three dimensions and the living practice of a faith. The doctrines, myths and so on cannot be properly understood save by reference to the

16

characteristic patterns of religious activity in the faith in question.

Thus Christianity involves the worship of God, the sacraments, etc. If God indeed were not to be worshipped would he be properly called 'God'? In some forms of religion, worship is rather unimportant, but other activities are more central. For example, in Theravada Buddhism there is no worship of the Buddha (though reverence is paid to the departed Teacher): what is central is the treading of the Path which culminates in the practice of contemplation. This contemplative life—yoga in the broad sense of the term—has its analogies to the contemplative life of Christian mystics, such as Suso or Ruysbroeck, even if its goal is interpreted very differently in Buddhism. But just as it is impossible to understand properly the concept of *God* or *sacrament* in Christian theology without entering at least imaginatively into the milieu of worship, so one cannot understand the idea of nirvana in Buddhism without entering at least imaginatively into the meditative life which takes one towards the goal. Since in the West we are more used to the religion of worship of God, and since worship is a form of ritual, I shall call this practical aspect of religion the *ritual dimension*.

To avoid misunderstanding, let me emphasize two points. First, I would not wish ritual to be confused with ritualism. The latter is an opprobrious term we sometimes use to designate ritual activities which have become merely mechanical or overelaborate. It is a disease afflicting religion when ritual is divorced from inner experience, from genuine concern, from religious sensitivity. Moreover, it is worth noting that ritual need not be elaborate: it can be very simple and informal. When I close my eyes in prayer, when a few are gathered together to sing a hymn—these are as much cases of ritual as a High Mass. Second, I want to include in the ritual dimension the contemplative practices to which I have referred in the case of Theravada Buddhism and Christian mysticism. This is perhaps artificial and a little strained. But mysticism is in the West treated as a form of prayer; and the function of contemplation in Buddhism, say, is analogous to the function of worship, etc. It is a response to and a quest for the transcendental world.

But we cannot fully appreciate religion or its meaning without paying attention to the inner life of those who are involved in the life of the dimensions we have so far considered. Indeed, many of the seminal moments of religious history have involved religious experiences of a dramatic kind: the Enlightenment of the Buddha, the vision of Isaiah in the Temple, the conversion of St. Paul, the prophecy of Muhammad—we could scarcely explain the directions religious history has taken without referring to such moments. At a humbler level there is the testimony of countless religious folk who believe themselves to have had moments of illumination, conversion, vision, a sense of presence and so on. We may refer to this aspect of religion as the *experiential dimension*.

Finally, though the continuance and development of religion may be nurtured internally (so to speak) by experience, they also depend on social institutions, such as the Church in Christianity and the Sangha in Buddhism. More widely, religion has its social roots and effects. All this can be referred to as the *social dimension* of religion.

Religion, then, has six dimensions, and in speaking of a religion we must bear in mind the fact that these dimensions are interrelated. Thus Christian worship is directed at a certain focus, the Trinity. The Trinity includes Christ. We cannot understand Christian worship without knowing its intention: prayer is more than shutting one's eyes. To understand the behaviour we must understand the concepts underlying it. And these concepts include those of *God* and *Christ*. It follows that the doctrinal and mythological dimensions of Christianity are necessary to the ritual. Again, the concept of love in Christianity involves the idea of reverence, itself intertwined with that of worship. Likewise it is impossible fully to understand the social institutions (the Church, or Churches) without attention to the doctrines which in theory control their life and organization. Again, the

18

understanding of religious experience (the sense of the birth of Christ in the soul, for instance) has in part to do with the way a person sees that experience. How can he see it as the birth of Christ in the soul without presupposing something of the doctrinal and mythological dimensions of Christianity?

The dimensions, then, are mutually dependent, though in different ways. They constitute a unity in plurality. Nevertheless, it is convenient for the moment to divide them into two groups. The first group consists in the doctrinal, mythological and ethical dimensions: the second group consists in the ritual, experiential and social dimensions. The ground for the division is this. The former group *par excellence* represents the parahistorical claims of the faith; while the latter group represents the phenomena of religious history in the world. We can concentrate on the conversion of Paul, the rise of the Church, the evolution of the sacraments. To understand these phenomena we need recourse to the other group, but still these things are the primary data of religion in the world. Conversely, when we come to systematize, parahistorically, the teachings of Christianity, we refer to the Creation, to the salvation-history of Israel, the commandments, etc. In short, we are more directly concerned with the first group of dimensions.

Thus we can say, by a crude simplification, that the first group verges towards the parahistorical, the second towards the historical. To understand the first group we must make reference to the second and conversely; but the first group has parahistorical primacy while the second has historical primacy. But let us immediately qualify this crudity.

Clearly the Church as a social institution is understood in terms of doctrine, and not merely this—the doctrines may be critical of it. The Christian theologian may evolve a view of the Church which is strongly at variance with the facts of ecclesiastical life. Thus he has a parahistorical (and not just a descriptive and historical) approach to the institution to which he himself belongs. In brief, a parahistorical treatment of the historical group is possible. Conversely, one can engage in the historical

19

treatment of doctrines, of mythology, of religious ethics. This is the other side of the coin. There can be a history of parahistory; just as there can be a parahistory of history.

Let me illustrate further. St. Augustine spent some effort in writing the *Civitas Dei*. This work was an interpretation of history as he knew it. It was a parahistorical approach to history. But those who write textbooks on political theory and the like are liable to give an historical account of Augustine's parahistory.

Thus the two groups of three have different primary relevances to religious and theological studies: but each group needs the other for its explication (no worship without doctrinal or mythological focus, no concept of God without reference to worship), and further there is an historical approach to the first group, and a parahistorical evaluation of the second.

Theology and religious studies need to bear these facts in mind if they are to escape unrealism, either by way of neglecting the religious milieu of theology or by way of neglecting the theological focus of religion.

Questions of religious truth, whether truth has simply and supposedly been presented in revelation, or whether it has been discussed philosophically or otherwise, have traditionally been important in education, and it is therefore vital that we should have some notion as to how one arrives at parahistorical truth. There are doubtless problems about historical, descriptive truth too: matters are not as easy, when one is dealing with cultural, anthropological matters such as religion, as might be thought. Still, there are in a way deeper problems about parahistory. How do we arrive at truth here? Or is 'arrived at' the wrong phrase? After all, faith is said to be God-given; and as was remarked earlier, theological and religious systems sometimes provide their own, internal criteria of truth. The way of coming to the truth would here depend on acceptance in the first instance of the truth of the system. The system thus becomes a closed system. But this is too formal a way of putting something which has a simpler and more direct expression. To say, for instance, that the truth about God (or the truth which is God) is given by

God is a way of saying that we ought to look to the self-revelation of God.

This in turn is a way of expressing a central tenet of Christianity in regard to its own commitment: namely that revelation comes from God. It is indeed hopeless to give any account of Christianity which omits revelation. Thus the problem, referred to earlier, of ideology—the problem of metaphysics—is in part (however modest a part) the problem of revelation. Does it make sense to believe in revelation?

But what is revelation? Here recent theology has made an important point, that we need to distinguish between revelation considered as the sentences contained in the scriptures and revelation considered as God's self-revelation in history, etc., and above all in Christ. The latter account of revelation is commonly called 'non-propositional'. But I would prefer to call it 'inductivist', in the sense that the Christian penetrates by a kind of induction through the sentences of the Bible to the events which constitute the revelation. By contrast, those who hold that revelation consists in the sentences of the Bible may be dubbed 'deductivists'—for they try to *deduce* the truth from the Bible, rather than to use the Bible as a stepping-stone to the truth. They treat scripture as authority: the other school treats it as evidence.

Now there is hardly a university theologian in the country who takes a strictly deductivist view. This is not surprising, because the cumulative impact of historical studies of the Bible over a hundred years and more renders the deductivist position largely untenable. Unfortunately, the Christian Church is saddled with this view in various forms. In this country, it flourishes most, however, among the Conservative Evangelicals. It flourishes too in a covert way among atheists and agnostics, who, in rejecting a deductivist version of Christianity, reject the Christian faith. Deductivism is probably a potent cause of the alienation of the liberal intellectual from the Christian tradition.

It is worth saying this, because too often in my own Church, the Church of England, public concern is expressed about the

21

way in which contemporary liberal theology, from *Soundings* onwards, may upset the faithful. Upsetting the faithless may, from the point of view of the Church, be much more damaging. And it has always seemed to me to be an odd paradox that those who are supposed to know the living God in personal experience and through the sacraments should be so upset by winds of theological and intellectual change. The paradox is like that found in the attempt on the part of those who supposedly know God already to try to prove his existence. I am sure a friend of mine would be a little upset if I kept trying to reassure myself that he really existed.

Perhaps all this has to do with the authenticity of religious conviction. The susceptibility of many Christians, and their ferocity towards those of different convictions, differ so markedly from the spirit of Jesus' teachings (remember: the good Samaritan was not orthodox in belief and practice) that it requires some explanation. Perhaps a parable may help. The Kingdom of Heaven is like treasure buried in a field. When a man finds it he covers it up and is so filled with joy that he goes and sells all he has and buys the field.* After that he builds a house over the treasure; but when he tells folk of his gold-mine they laugh at him. So he hires witnesses to testify that it is real gold. Folk think that this must show that it can't be the real thing. The man gets angry, and sits on his porch every evening, with a machine-gun, to protect his gold.

However, it is understandable that the inductivist approach to revelation should raise apprehensions. It means that there is room both for scepticism about how historical the Gospels are and for the infiltration of present fashions into the interpretation of revelation. On the first score, we have the example of Rudolf Bultmann, who in effect has abandoned the quest for the historical Jesus: the experience of the Church, beginning with that of the disciples, which is symbolized by the story of the resurrection, is central to the Christian message. Behind those experi-

* *The Four Gospels*, translated by E. V. Rieu, Penguin Books, London, 1952, p. 75.

ences, the historical person of Jesus quietly evaporates. On the second score, we have the example of the liberal theology of the period before the First World War, which too easily identified the Gospel with ideas of social and moral progess. It is the great achievement of Karl Barth to hammer home the possibility that our doctrinal reconstructions are merely projections which cover up the God-given revelation in Christ.

But it is worth noting that human presuppositions and emotions can quite as easily creep into the deductivist's interpretation of scripture as into the inductivist's. For the Southern Baptist in the United States the scriptures can justify racial inequality; while for many missionaries in countries once dominated by the colonial powers the scriptures said the opposite thing (it was not for nothing that the East India Company did not want missionaries in the territories under its control—and the examples of Rhodesia and South Africa also show how the Gospel can be politically explosive). Again, the teetotaller sometimes justifies his (perhaps on other grounds justifiable) abstention by appeal to the scriptures, even if Jesus is recorded as having turned water into wine rather than wine into water. These are instances of the degree to which the interpreters of scripture can disagree, though sharing a deductivist standpoint. Thus the dangers of inductivism are reflected also in a different way in deductivism. But in any case I shall for the rest of my argument assume the correctness of the inductive approach, which is, among other things, more exciting and fruitful educationally. Perhaps I can explain my standpoint by a further parable, which owes something to an image used in Eastern thought (the non-propositional view of revelation is found in traditional Indian teaching):

A blind boy is told by his uncle about the shape and beauty of the moon. The moon, says his uncle, is perfectly smooth and made of shining silver. It lights up the night and is an assurance for those who travel in the dark. One day, by a miracle, the boy is healed of his blindness. He gradually accustoms himself to the new world of sight, and he sees the heavenly moon. He is so overjoyed he buys the latest invention, a telescope. He sees that the moon is cratery, and can scarcely be made of silver. He tells his uncle, but does not complain. 'Dear Uncle,' he says, 'you were the first to tell me of the beauties of the moon. Without you I would perhaps never have looked to see it, craters and all. Indeed it is beautiful, though it is not made of silver. Who cares? I like the moon as it is: it is more wonderful than even your words suggested.'

Yet something remains obscure about the inductivist approach. To what is it that we penetrate through the scriptural records? Is it just the historical events—such as that Jesus died on the cross? But the historical events by themselves need not be revelatory. Both the Christian and the sceptic will agree that Jesus was crucified: but the sceptic will not confer the title 'revelatory' upon the event. Already the very term 'revelation' is bringing a religious or theological category to bear upon what is perceived.

Some theologians nowadays use the expression 'the Christ-event'. It is a useful shorthand for the part of the history of salvation constituted by the life and acts of Jesus. Let us then, for convenience' sake, concentrate on that major element in revelation summed up as the Christ-event. Now here we are not just concerned, as I have indicated, with the historical facts of Jesus' life: these are seen, by the Christian, both as revelatory and as bringing something obscurely called salvation to mankind. To speak of the Christ-event is already to make a parahistorical affirmation. It is somehow to this that scripture is supposed to bear witness. If we can elucidate something of the logic of this language of the Christ-event, we shall no doubt have a better understanding of what revelation is supposed to be.

Here we can revert to our six dimensions, for part of that analysis may help to clarify the nature of the Christ-event. Let us first consider, in relation to those dimensions, the very idea that the Christ-event is revelatory. This presupposes that there is something more than Jesus who is revealed in Jesus. Of course it is just possible that all that Jesus reveals is himself: but then

24

he is just a human figure, and as such is no more revelatory than Socrates or John Stuart Mill. Both these last revealed themselves, no doubt. Rather, the Christian idea of revelation implies that there is a transcendent holy Being who reveals himself in Christ. Consequently, to use the category of revelation it is already necessary to have a doctrine of God. The concept of revelation to this extent belongs to the doctrinal dimension of Christianity.

But second, the locus of the revelation is in the Christ-event, and that by definition involves the life and acts of the historical Jesus. To this extent, the application of the idea of revelation in Christianity belongs to the mythological dimension.

But what is revealed is necessarily revealed in principle *to* someone. It is paradoxically absurd to say 'I have just revealed the secret of the Dead Sea Scrolls, but to no one.' Likewise, religious revelation implies a target: in particular, human beings. The story of the transfiguration of Jesus is a good illustration of what is meant, however we may interpret the details of the account. Suddenly Jesus is revealed *to* Simon Peter as a Messianic figure. Thus revelation in its human aspect belongs to the experiential dimension of religion, and is reciprocated by the worship and prayer that such a revelation calls forth. For the purposes of our argument, though the ritual, ethical and social dimensions enter in in various ways to the response to revelation and into its continuance through the life of the community stemming from the initial revelation, we can concentrate upon the experiential side, as far as human response goes.

Thus the Christ-event can be considered in three dimensions— doctrinal, mythological and experiential. The Christ-event has to be understood by reference to the category of transcendence, the category of historical events, and the category of the experience of the faithful. For the sake of simplicity, I shall dub the transcendent aspect of the Christ-event 'the transcendent Christ'; the historical aspect I shall dub 'the historical Jesus' and the experiential aspect I shall call 'the existential Christ'.

I shall now attempt to confirm this analysis by considering the odd results which we get from missing out one of these dimen-

sions. Various forms of two-dimensional Christs do not correspond to the tradition, and in other ways they show defects. (For
it might be thought, rightly, that a mere appeal to tradition is
not enough: at best it serves the purpose of defining traditional
Christian belief.)

There has in recent times been a notable exposition of a two-
dimensional Christianity in the shape of Paul van Buren's *The
Secular Meaning of the Gospel*. This work has various ancestors,
among them alleged analyses of religious language (such as those
of R. B. Braithwaite and I. T. Ramsey) and the writings of Bultmann. Like Braithwaite, van Buren dispenses with the notion of
a transcendent Creator; but unlike Braithwaite, he takes the
historical events of Jesus' life seriously. Moreover, while Braithwaite considered the heart of Christianity to be loving (aga-
peistic) behaviour, as illuminated by the Christian parables, van
Buren incorporates the existential side of Bultmann. Jesus is
saviour, for his freedom and authentic existence are contagious:
they carry over into our lives today, and we can partake in that
authenticity. Thus the Christian is one who views the world
from the perspective of the historical events of Jesus' life, and is
gripped by the experience of true freedom. In my terms: the
Christ-event of van Buren consists only in the historical Jesus
and in the existential Christ.

This means, as van Buren implicitly concedes, that it is hard
or impossible to justify the choice of perspective: others might
find Socrates and the Buddha more liberating and contagious
examples. The uniqueness of the Christ-event is thus not easily
if at all defensible on the van Buren analysis. On the other hand,
the three-dimensional Christ is identified, certainly at the transcendent level, with a divine Being who is held on other grounds
to be uniquely the Creator and sustainer of the universe. In
brief, van Buren's two-dimensional Christ is hardly more than a
hero. And there is no special call to be loyal to a single hero
above all other heroes.

Further, men worship Christ: but why worship someone who
is not strictly speaking God, because not transcendent? Belief in

providence and other features of faith in a Creator likewise evaporate.

Another two-dimensional Christ is that yielded by subtracting the historical Jesus. In effect, this is what happens according to Bultmann's theology. As I remarked before, the emphasis in Bultmann, because of his scepticism about the possibility of reconstructing the historical Jesus, is upon the existential Christ. The experience of the early Church is called in to redress the balance upset by the disappearance of Jesus.

The trouble with this view is that it makes history irrelevant to the truth of Christianity. Provided the disciples and Paul had an experience of the risen Lord, it matters not who Jesus claimed to be or how he acted. Moreover, there is no special reason to exclude from our view the existential experiences of other faiths. Naturally we should not do so in any event: but the problem of other faiths becomes insoluble on Bultmann's doctrine, save by saying that in various ways the divine Being manifests himself in religious experience. Indeed, in some respects Eastern religions must have the edge over Christianity, for they are much more concerned to stress the experiential dimension of faith. But of course this argument against Bultmann only works on the assumption that it is a specifically Christian theology which we want to defend. Thus far we are merely, in effect, appealing to tradition.

But a more radical criticism is that Bultmann can scarcely make sense of the early Christian experience itself: for the Gospels amply demonstrate their concern with at least some aspects of the life of the historical Jesus, while the Creed slips in the phrase 'under Pontius Pilate' to bring out the dated, historical, flesh-and-blood nature of the person in whom the early Church had faith.

Another two-dimensional Christ is found by subtracting the existential Christ. Suppose we believe in the historical Jesus, and in a transcendent God, but not in the possibility of a living relationship to Christ here and now, we have a unitarian doctrine. Now Unitarianism is a respectable faith: all that can be

27

said, then, is that it is not Christian, and cannot fully make sense of the scriptures. Unitarianism as it has grown out of Christendom has thus tended to suffer from the weakness that it has concentrated upon the New Testament, when it should also have taken the *Bhagavadgītā* and various other documents into account.

Alternatively, if we identify Jesus with God, but deny the possibility of a living relationship with him, we are landed with an abstract and, so to say, useless Deity, rather like the gods of Epicurus, who never have traffic with men. A God who does not reveal himself is indeed a strange Being, for he nowhere appears in the context of religion. Such a Being may exist, but it would be pointless speculating about it.

If, then, two-dimensional Christs suffer from inherent defects, so much the more do the various versions of a one-dimensional Christ.

I conclude therefore that revelation—that which the Christian tries to penetrate to through the words of scripture—must have this three-dimensional character. This means that a para-historical inquiry into revelation must concern itself with arguments about the concept of transcendence, arguments about historical facts and arguments about religious experience. No completely rich theology can neglect these three areas.

I shall argue that the first of these concerns inevitably involves us both in doctrinal affirmations and philosophical questions. Hence the philosophy of religion is a necessary component of a rich theology. I shall argue that the second of these concerns is not specialized, but is part of history in general. This in turn means that there is a limit on the degree of *a priori* reasoning in theology. I shall argue that the third of these concerns involves us necessarily in comparative studies. Through all this, we may detect a strange light glimmering, a light which shows us how the paradox of theology in a secular university can be resolved. For the philosophy of religion, the history of the Jews and the comparative study of religion are only particular branches of philosophy, history and anthropology.

But it is not enough to say that these approaches are necessary. It is desirable too to illustrate them concretely. I therefore wish to engage in three arguments in the next three chapters: a philosophical and doctrinal argument about the notion of Creation, which will have much to do with the concept of transcendence and will illustrate something of the fundamental issues of systematic theology and its relation to science; an historical argument about the enigmatic figure of Barabbas—an argument which will I hope bring out something of the temper of historical studies of the New Testament; and an argument about the relation between religious experience and ritual, which will illustrate the relevance of the comparative study of religion to the concerns of Christian parahistory.

In the last chapter I shall attempt to show how the methodological considerations resulting from these examples should direct religious studies in their various embodiments in educational institutions.

This is no doubt an overbold programme. It is especially bold for me in at least one respect. My training, such as it is, has been mainly in philosophy and in the comparative study of religion, with especial reference to Indian religions. I cannot claim to be a New Testament scholar, except by dim anticipation. But it seems to me that it is not enough to talk about what should be done: it is also necessary to do it by example. And it is better to be excited than repetitive of the thoughts of others. It happens that I have a theory about an aspect of New Testament history, which colleagues tell me is not at all implausible by comparison with other theories. And as James Barr, that notorious cat among Old Testament pigeons, has recently written: 'It is doubtful if anyone who has not faced the fact of historical criticism has begun to see the point of modern theology.'*

To recapitulate: religious studies have two aspects, the historical or descriptive on the one hand; and the parahistorical on the other. Religion, the object of such studies, has six dimen-

* Daniel Jenkins (ed.), *The Scope of Theology*, Cleveland, Ohio, 1965, p. 27.

sions—the doctrinal, mythological, ethical, ritual, experiential and social. The first three form a group verging towards the parahistorical: the latter three a group verging towards the historical. But there can be history of parahistory as well as parahistory of history. Christian theology, as parahistory, is concerned at least with revelation, which thus has some modest relevance to questions of ideology and metaphysics. Revelation can be considered either inductively or deductively. The approach here is the former. A primary segment of revelation, from the point of view of Christian parahistory and from the point of view of inductivism, is the Christ-event. This must be considered as at least three-dimensional—interpreted in terms of doctrine (i.e. the concept of a transcendent Being), mythology (i.e. the historical Jesus), and experience (i.e. the existential Christ). By consequence a completely rich theology must involve the philosophy of religion, historical studies and the comparative study of religion. And, as we shall see, philosophy needs doctrines to bite on.

CHAPTER II

CREATION AND GALILEO GALILEI

I wish here to propound an argument which I hope will show something of the relations between Christian doctrine, philosophy and science. I wish to illustrate the relations through a consideration of the idea of the Creation of the world by God.

This is, I think, a doctrine which retains a perennial interest, whether we believe it or not, for it touches in one way on the very fringes of our knowledge and in another on the very heart of our existence. It touches on the fringes, because it seems to have something to do with speculative cosmology. The extraordinarily immense and rich cosmos revealed by astronomical investigations in this century and the plethora of theorizing about the nature and origin of the universe belong to a truly exciting frontier of physical knowledge and speculation, and we feel that somehow these matters bear rather strongly upon the idea of Creation. And the latter idea touches the heart of our existence because the story of Creation in *Genesis* ties it quite closely in with what some have called the special creation of the human species. The doctrine, then, seems to have implications for both cosmology and biology.

Nevertheless, we may experience a certain uneasiness about this way of looking at it. *Genesis*, after all, expresses itself somewhat poetically. It has not the style of a scientific treatise. And is not the idea of Creation in part at least a means of expressing a sense of dependence on, and gratitude to, God? This is far from a speculative or theoretical attitude. Thus we can easily conclude that the idea of Creation belongs rather to the realm of

31

faith and religion, and not to the realm of (so to say) objective truth.

These two rather different feelings about the idea of Creation correspond to two special traps which people are forever liable to tumble into. The first error is to treat the doctrine as a bit of super-science. The second is to treat it just existentially. Deductivists are more liable to tumble into the former trap; and inductivists into the latter, partly because theology has in recent times been so much influenced by Existentialism (but a similar trend is found among those influenced by what purport to be philosophical analyses of religion). I wish to show that a combination of hard-headed criticism and philosophical thinking is necessary if anything is to be made of the doctrine. It will follow from this that philosophizing is a necessary component of parahistorical inquiry into doctrine. In other words, it is not possible to base theology upon an exclusive appeal to revelation, whether this be conceived from a deductive or from an inductive point of view.

This conclusion, if correct, is of such profound importance that it is perhaps in order for me to describe briefly an extraordinary phenomenon in recent theological thinking which the conclusion essentially is hostile to.

Those who are sceptical about Christianity may see in the phenomenon another instance of the ponderous *naïveté* of so many Christian scholars. Yet there are forms of *naïveté* elsewhere, let it be said.

The phenomenon in question is the rise of what has been loosely called 'Biblical Theology'. Scholars, having abandoned deductivism and a propositional view of revelation, because of the results of historical and other criticism, are, if they are strong Protestants, in a difficult position. For one main strand in Protestant thinking has been the idea that the Bible is the sole source of true doctrine about God. How can theology remain exclusively Biblical in the new context of historical criticism? This is the problem. The solution of Biblical Theology is to say that the key categories and events of the Bible, judging from the tenor of the Bible considered as a unitary whole, themselves form the basis and substance of theological truth. Consequently the task of theology is to lay bare the significance of these categories and events and to order them into a systematic exposition. The categories of the Bible, then, are taken for granted.

Biblical Theology in this sense tries also to show that there is something highly idiosyncratic about the Biblical way of looking at things. In particular, since Biblical Theologians disapprove of importing philosophical ideas into theology (this is a disapproval in part stemming from Karl Barth's onslaught on liberal theology), there is an attempt to show how different Biblical thought was from the thought of the Greek environment into which Christianity spread—and Greek thought of course is allegedly rather philosophical. Hence it is a ghastly commonplace of Biblical Theology that Hebrew thought differs profoundly from Greek. As for the New Testament, which embarrassingly enough is written in Greek, it is essentially permeated with Hebrew-style attitudes.

The net result of Biblical Theology is to substitute for the revelation of propositions the revelation of categories. For the history of salvation, as manifested in historical events such as the Exodus and the death and resurrection of Jesus, can only be understood as such through the categories in question. Since a lot of imagery is used in the Bible, and since the term 'categories' sounds as though it refers to abstract ideas, a variant of the position is to treat *images* as the substance of revelation.

Now in one way this approach has a certain force on its side. If revelation is to be a necessary component of Christian belief— if it is to be the data or part of the data on which Christianity bases its view of the world—then it does not seem to be right to be totally critical of the Bible. Yes, some of the historical facts may be open to question; yes, some of the mythology, especially where it bears on cosmology, may be wrong; yes, Paul's attitudes and doctrines may not be absolutely the word of God—all this we can say. But if we call in question the key ways of interpreting events and experience as contained in the Bible, revelation will surely dissolve into dust. It will dissolve, because a mere recital of neat historical events about Jesus or Jeremiah will mean nothing without the sort of interpretation placed upon them in the Biblical documents. This is the objection.

The reply to the objection is this. The interpretation of events is, in its way, an exercise in human imagination. It propounds, if you like, a poetry and a theory of those events. This poetry and theory partly arise from prophetic and other experience. For instance, Paul's interpretation of Christianity surely stems in great measure from his personal experience on the Damascus Road and elsewhere. It is absurd for us to reject interpretation of this sort in advance. Such interpretation is creative. We therefore treat it as given, though not thereby infallible. It is given because it stems from experience and a close imagination. It is not infallible for the same reason (or much the same reason) that new insights elsewhere are not infallible.

Einstein's theories of relativity (the special and the general) involve an imaginative use of the human intellect which goes beyond the current data and theories. We do not look askance because of this latter fact. But we still may wish, and ought to wish, to test Einstein. Much the same can be said about the categories of revelation. They are given; but they are not infallible. It is through a dialectic which starts with the Biblical categories and the historical events that we may come to an apprehension of the truth. In this sense, Biblical Theology is (to adopt the late J. L. Austin's words) a begin-all but not necessarily an end-all. Since it is treated so often by its exponents as an end-all it is to this extent foolish. This point will, I hope, become clearer as we proceed.

Now the Creation story in *Genesis* is a saga which carries on into the story of God's dealings with men. It is, so to say, continuous with the historical narrative which forms the main substance of the Old Testament. It thus has a close connection with the story of the Covenant; it also has a ritual dimension, for it involves an explanation of the ritual requirements for observing the Sabbath. The story as we have it reflects the achievements of prophetic movement, in stimulating and reinforcing the mono-theistic faith of Old Testament Judaism. Because of the con-nection in the Old Testament between creation and the history of salvation, it seems as though the beginning of the world is woven intimately into the course of human events.

This impression is reinforced by the fact that a special place in the saga is assigned to the creation of man and his subsequent disobedience.

It is not therefore altogether surprising that the Creation saga should have come to be interpreted rather literally. On the face of it there is no difference in category between, say, Moses and Noah, nor between Noah and Adam. If Moses belongs to history, then Adam does too. And if the story of Adam is to be taken thus literally, so is the story of his creation by God.

Now admittedly, once we probe deeper into the texts, we detect a strongly mythological flavour to the story of Adam: at one level it may have been stated as an account of part of the chronicle of mankind—but at another level, Adam is a symbol of mankind, and the tale of his disobedience expresses a continuing sense of the rupture between men and God. The story as originally written contained a mixture of the literal and symbolic, and typifies a state of culture in which the distinctions which *we* make between history, mythology, doctrine, etc., were scarcely made, save perhaps implicitly.

This fact of the undifferentiated character of so much scrip-tural writing brings me to the first and vital thesis I wish to propound: *the Bible itself does not lay bare the principles upon which it is to be interpreted.*

It follows that anyone attempting to write a Biblical Theology two hundred years ago could have said: 'It is a key idea in the Bible that God speaks to men through historical events; tracing the story back we come to the tale of Adam; it can thus be seen that part of the Biblical message is the affirmation that the first member of the human race fell into disobedience through the eating of a forbidden fruit. It could be further argued that part of the Biblical message is that man is a special creation of God in a way in which the animals are not, namely by the breathing of a soul or spirit into man.'

We know the consequences of this type of approach to scripture. By the time we finish, the story of Adam ends up as a thesis in biology which is incompatible with the full acceptance of the theory that men are (both physically and psychologically) descended from animals. But the very fact that the story of Adam no longer fits easily or at all into the framework of knowledge supplied by palaeontology, prehistory and biology, is, of course, one of the factors which may help to remind us that the story of Adam must at best be given a symbolic significance. In brief, modern knowledge itself is a factor in the shaping of our interpretation of the Bible. It is an illusion to suppose that the Biblical categories are untouched by changes in our outlook upon the world.

Now the idea that the Adam story and the Creation saga are not to be treated as bits of biology and cosmology is bound to lead some people to some sort of dualism between religious and scientific concepts. It is bound to lead to some such view as this : that the stories in *Genesis* are statements of, or expressions of, faith, whereas scientific theories, etc., have a different role to play. Such a view can be put crudely by saying : the language of religion has a different style from the language of science. This seems an excellent conclusion.

Nevertheless, language, as well as having a style, has a reference. Thus, the statement that Christ died for our sins may unmistakably bear the style of a religious claim (for it uses the concepts of *Christ* and *sins*), but it surely refers to an historical event, namely the death of Jesus. But to what is it that the story of Creation refers?

The relations between styles and references open up various ways in which we can roughly characterize some possible and actual philosophical or theological positions. One possibility is to say that the reference of scientific and religious utterances is the same, but the styles are different. If you like, they express two ways of looking at the same thing. This possibility itself breaks down into others, according as we characterize the difference in styles.

Thus on the one hand we may hold that the scientific style is essentially descriptive and explanatory, and that the religious style is expressive, emotive, etc. If we take this view, the doctrine of Creation is a means of expressing a reaction to or attitude to the world. This position is that of Paul van Buren in his *The Secular Meaning of the Gospel*. Unfortunately, we now no longer have a use for the utterance 'There is a God' to express a possible reference for religious assertions, for there is no being over and above the cosmos. We may thus characterize this position as 'the thesis of pious atheism'.

Alternatively we may hold that though the reference of religious and scientific utterances is the same, nevertheless there are different aspects of empirical reality which the different styles serve to describe or evoke. A parallel might be the person: for we can ascribe both physical and psychological predicates to the same being, namely a person, and they seem to belong to rather different styles of discourse. Because of this parallel, and because there seems a strong existential element in revelation, this parallel is sometimes taken very seriously. In so far as the cosmos displays personal characteristics, we can use the religious style; in so far as it can be treated impersonally, we use the scientific. Now the world certainly contains persons, but this cannot be a sufficient reference for religious utterances, if we take the concept of God seriously. Thus this position either collapses into a variant of pious atheism, or it attempts to treat the cosmos as somehow personal. This is, seemingly,* the move made by Ian Ramsey, when he talks in his *Religious Language* and elsewhere of the cosmos 'coming alive in a personal way'. If, then, we hold that there is an identity of reference, but a difference in styles, to bring out different aspects of reality, we hold a position which can be dubbed 'the thesis of pious pantheism'.

* Only seemingly; I refer the reader to discussions in *Theology*, the January 1965 issues and its successors. But if my Ian Ramsey does not exist, it would be necessary to invent him.

Before going on to characterize other views, let us see the defects of the former two positions. The thesis of pious atheism has the drastic consequence that the ritual dimension of religion —worship and prayer—has no more than a ceremonial significance. Thus the logic of religious activity is, so to say, destroyed. Moreover it is no longer possible to look on Christ as anything more than the hero, Jesus. There are not wanting those who would not shrink from this drastic conclusion; but it means the wholesale destruction of Biblical categories, and thus the ultimate destruction of the notion of revelation itself. It is thus incompatible with Christianity as hitherto understood, and so deserves a different name. 'Pious atheism' seems as good a one as any.

Nevertheless, a partially relevant reply may be made. It may be said that it can only be characterized as atheism because it does not affirm 'God exists'. Now this may not be a genuine religious-style utterance in any case. Thus Tillich has claimed that we can no longer sensibly ask 'Does God exist?', while funtionalist theologians such as van Peursen claim that Biblical language is essentially relational and dynamic, in always speaking of God's acts in relation to men, etc., and not ontological. Now this is thought of in relation to the contrast between Hebrew and Greek thought; but it also might be thought to be relevant to the statement 'God exists', which possibly is a candidate for the obscure title 'ontological'. But these points do not add up to much. Tillich's point boils down to the trivial remark that God is not a being in space and time, so we cannot use 'exists' of him. But classically God has not been thought of as being in space and time, so the affirmation of his existence has not been taken to imply this. The functionalist point need scarcely detain us, for it is obvious that to ascribe activity to a person is to presuppose his existence. We may thus conclude that pious atheism cannot be represented as essentially in line with mainstream religious-style language.

The thesis of pious pantheism has the disadvantage that it must find it hard to express what the Creation story means. For the fact that the cosmos may be found to have a personal flavour to it on occasions does not at all show that it owes its existence to the personal aspect. Far from it: *ex hypothesi* the cosmos is identical with God.

We now turn to the third main possibility: namely that both the styles and references of scientific and religious language are different. We might, for instance, hold that religious discourse is about God and scientific discourse about the cosmos (or about bits thereof). Let us sharpen this possibility up by supposing that there is no overlap at all. This bifurcation, of course, scarcely can be a representation of Biblical language, which is so much about God's historical acts in relation to men. Nor can it help in exhibiting the meaning of the doctrine of Creation, for this has something to do with the cosmos.

A more promising version of the possibility is that religious-style language has reference to God and to the world (or events in the world) in so far as it stands in relation to God, while scientific discourse is about the world (or bits of the world) considered in itself. Let me use an illustration. We might have York-language, which is about York, and about Canterbury in so far as Canterbury stands in relation to York. Likewise there is God-language, which is about God and the world in so far as it is related to God; while scientific language is about the cosmos (or bits of it) considered in itself. As we shall see, this version of the relation between religious and scientific discourse has one or two variants. But immediately it raises a problem.

The problem is this: why should a difference in reference require a difference in style? For instance, I may use colour concepts to describe the scene in my garden. If I now turn my attention to some nearby factory chimneys, there is a new possible reference for my colour concepts. I do not need to use a different style of talking in order to describe the visual appearance of the chimneys. In brief, we need to understand why the fact that religious language refers to God should force it to be of a different style from scientific language.

Different attempts have been made to solve this problem. The most popular one is to stress the personal character of God. Given a kind of Existentialist doctrine, one can then go on to claim that scientific language is adapted to dealing with what is impersonal, while a different kind of language is needed to express subjective experience and inter-personal relations. Thus the language of religion is essentially to do with the relations between God and men. It also has a bearing on the way people react to the world—to death, for example.

Now the Existentialist explanation itself contains a great problem. For it appears to confine religious language to an expression of the communication between God and men. It is thus liable to take a form in which the doctrine of Creation itself becomes an expression of this relationship, or perhaps also an expression of the kind of reaction we should have to the world (to treat it as good, etc.). But then it no longer seems to be the doctrine that the cosmos actually owes its existence to and depends continuously upon God's activity. Thus this variant of the position can be dubbed 'the thesis of restricted theism'. It is restricted, since it is compatible with God's being a finite personal being who enters into revelatory relationships with men. Such restricted theism is for this reason always liable to anthropomorphism. Yet it is attractive as a way of expounding the real meaning of the scriptures, since as we saw, the Creation narrative is placed in such close relationship to the later historical interplay between God and Israel.

The only way, it seems, to avoid the thesis of restricted theism if one sticks to the Existentialist explanation of the relations between science and religion is to claim that a kind of intersubjective or 'I-Thou' relationship to the cosmos is possible. Martin Buber and Karl Heim have not shrunk from some such claim. We can dub this 'the thesis of panpsychism'. But this has the disadvantage (apart from its paradoxicality) that the real motive for the theist in wanting to go beyond restricted theism is that he wants to affirm the dependence of everything in the world upon God, whether or not we are capable of entering into any kind of existential relationship with trees and the like. This relation of dependence is, for the theist, not simply a way of expressing one's attitude to inanimate things; but is the conceptual basis of a proper attitude.

There are other objections to what I have called the Existentialist solution to the problem of reference. The notion that scientific inquiry essentially concerns the impersonal aspects of reality is intolerably crude, as witness the advances being made in the biological sciences. But there is no need or space to go into this side of the problem. Yet though the Existentialist solution suffers from defects, it is a partial answer. For part of the reason for the characteristic style of Christian religious language is that it refers primarily to a personal being, namely God, and endeavours to express the appropriate reactions of the faithful to that Person.

Another solution to the problem we can dub 'the range-of-experience solution'. The idea is this: just as the language of musical criticism has its special concepts, etc., so too the language of religion. The former style arises from the nature of musical experience; the latter from the nature of religious experience. Thus the fact that religious language refers to a special range of experience imposes upon it a special style. An important attempt to delineate the character of the range of religious experience was Rudolf Otto's *The Idea of the Holy*. This approach is in some degree fruitful, for it connects up religious concepts to such activities as worship through which a reaction to the experience of the holy is expressed. It thus helps to give an intelligible account of the relation between the experiential and ritual dimensions of religion.

But the range-of-experience solution is, again, only partial. For musical experience is one aspect of our life and (so to say) no more. Why should not religious experience be treated in the same way? But then at best the doctrine of Creation expresses a sense of awe. The attempted solution is compatible with a finite God (perhaps constituted by all the religious experiences which men have had and will have).

But as I have said, it is at least a partial solution. Because it brings in the ritual dimension of religion, it is liable to lead to a better appraisal of the expressive and performative aspects of religious language, unduly neglected in the past. This has had some fruitful consequences, such as the Austinian analysis of religious language in Donald Evans' excellent *The Logic of Self-Involvement*. Nevertheless, if the expressive and performative side is over-stressed we get just another form of pious atheism, though it is rather more pious than the other form mentioned above.

So far the solutions amount to saying this: religious language has its special character because it expresses a relationship between a personal and holy being on the one hand and men on the other. But, as we have seen, this partial solution is compatible with belief in a finite God on whom the world does not depend. The logic of the situation drives us beyond these partial solutions.

The style of Christian and theistic language must owe something to the fact that it makes reference to a transcendent being —a being who is distinct from the cosmos, and is thus not a spatial entity. Such a being, in so far as he is Creator, is not to be conceived as the explanation of a single event, namely the coming into being of the cosmos, but as the continuous sustainer of the world. The doctrine implies that invisibly God is, so to say, behind all events, invisibly, though liable to manifest himself through particular events. Such is the traditional theistic concept of a transcendent being.

Our solution then is this: the style of Christian religious language is in part due to the personal nature of God; but this personhood is not human, as religious experience testifies; and it is not material, as the concept of transcendence makes plain. For a double reason, it does not come within the purview of science. But not because science is inadequate. Only because things are as they are. That is the claim of theism.

Let me exhibit what I mean by a parable.

There was a man brought up in a room. It was a strange room, for one wall manifested a constantly changing picture—a scene of jungle trees and prowling animals under a tropical moon and star-sprinkled deep blue sky. The man watched the scene. Occasionally to his surprise its left-hand part was obliterated by a patch of light which spoke, and he sometimes conformed his actions to what the voice said. He became fond of the occasional light.

Friends dropped in. They had different theories. One said there might be something behind the wall. 'That is what I've long thought,' said the man. Another said that there was nothing behind the wall, but the light must be taken seriously. He represented pious atheism. Another said that it wasn't the light that spoke but the whole wall. It was the wall that spoke—the whole wall, he insisted. He represented pious pantheism. Another said that there was a fellow behind the light. He represented the thesis of restricted theism. Another said that there was a fellow behind the light, and that the trees and animals were fellows too. And the moon. He represented panpsychism.

Still another said that the fellow behind the light and the voice was also behind the trees and animals and moon and stars. It was he that projected them all on to the wall.

He got upset when another friend came in and said. 'Behind? There's no behind. There's a wall. You can show that there are correlations between events shown on the wall. You can explain them that way. There are colleagues who insist on talking about underlying bricks to explain the phenomena. But apart from that you can't talk about anything behind. Certainly not behind the wall.'

The man got depressed by this and tried to stick to the view that there was just a light and a voice and a wall. But he got no satisfaction. For he really believed in the fellow behind.

This last part of the parable reflects the curious situation in contemporary philosophy and theology. The positivistic doctrine that factual claims can have no reference to a transcendent being has so impressed itself on religious thinking that the main trend in the alleged analysis of religious utterances has been towards pious atheism, pious pantheism and in general a subjectivist interpretation of religious 'truth'. Thus the premiss that

43

the doctrine of creation is not scientific has led to the unwarranted conclusion, in effect, that it is not a doctrine at all.

The notion of a holy, personal being who creatively sustains the cosmos is admittedly not a scientific one; for it refers to something which is not open to observational or experimental probing; nor does the concept help in any way as a constituent of scientific hypotheses or theories. It is indeed important for the understanding of Christianity that attempts to make God into a kind of scientific hypothesis, either in regard to the beginning of the world or in regard to the emergence of man, have run counter to the evidence and to the theoretical assumptions of scientists. In this way scientific advance contributes positively to the proper interpretation of Christianity. Without this advance it is highly likely that religion would still be encumbered with inaccurate and fallacious conceptions of cosmology and prehistory. In practice, therefore, scientific criticism of alleged interpretations of revelation which make pseudo-scientific claims is itself a necessary constituent in the pursuit of religious truth. Thus it is unsatisfactory to rest doctrine on a purely theological interpretation of the scriptures, which is likely not to take such necessary criticism into account.

But this liberation of theism from the encumbrances of a God of the gaps (a God, incidentally who belongs essentially to the scientific age: for gaps in scientific knowledge necessarily postdate the rise of scientific knowledge)—this liberation does not at all entail that God cannot be an explanation of the existence of the cosmos. It does not at all entail that there is no metaphysical level at which it is sensible to say that the cosmos depends on God.

Thus the existence of the cosmos itself requires explanation, in so far as it might not exist and might not have existed. Since scientific explanations, to put the matter crudely, explain features of the cosmos in terms of other features of the cosmos, an explanation of the existence of the cosmos as a whole necessarily goes beyond the type of explanation found in science. This fact has, of course, laid the doctrine open to the criticism that it

44

claims to be an explanation while not being a scientific explanation, and so is unintelligible.

But this criticism may be countered when we remember that the doctrine of Creation is not simply the affirmation that there is an underlying Cause of the cosmos: it is not a bare and mysterious claim of that kind. Rather it is the doctrine that the world continuously depends upon something analogous to a personal act of will. That is, the doctrine, as used in the context of theism, involves the notion of a personal being on whom the world depends.

Thus it is a richer notion than that of a First Cause, for the Creator is both personal and accessible to religious experience. He is also, from the Christian point of view, operative in particular historical events. But let me here concentrate upon the personal character of the Creator. This means that the charge that the type of explanation of the existence of the world used in theology is unintelligible can be rebutted.

It can be rebutted because there is an analogy to personal explanations: for instance, 'He shot him down because he had come to the conclusion that he was a dangerous lunatic.' This explanation of how a bullet came to lodge in the heart of the victim is not a simple physical explanation, for it makes use of the notion of a personal cause. In so far as such personal explanations do not enter into cosmology, the analogy between personal explanations and the doctrine of Creation shows that here we have moved into a different style of discourse. The use of the personal analogy then has two golden merits: first, it gives some content to the explanation, and second it shows that the explanation is not supposed to belong to the sphere of the physical sciences. It rebuts the charge of unintelligibility while at the same time preserving the doctrine from degeneration into pseudo-scientific cosmology. But here another criticism, more subtle perhaps, will be advanced. It is that there is a fudging in the doctrine. God is treated as personal, but at the same time is treated as non-spatial, transcendent, infinite—while persons as we know them are in space, are not transcendent beings, are

45

not infinite. In short, God is said to be a person, and yet is not literally a person. The concept, the criticism runs, gains its power from pretending to be the ordinary one, but is used in a context where it cannot be the ordinary one. It is thus a bit of pseudo-talk, pretending to be respectable but secretly withdrawing all the grounds of respectability.

The answer to this is to say: Yes, indeed, the concept of the person is used in a special way in relation to God. It is used analogically. (Conversely, the predicate *holy* is applied to God, and this is used literally, while when you say that a child is a holy terror you use it analogically.) But what's wrong with analogies? Without it science would never have progressed. Are radio waves really liquid? Are ova really eggs? Are quantum-jumps really jumps? Is energy energy? Is force force? Is a field a field? Is gravitational attraction attraction? Is inertia inertia? Is mass mass? Is natural selection selection? Is continuous creation creation? Is curved space curved? Is a projection a projection? Is a genetic code a code? Need I go on?

But it will be answered that the theories which incorporate these analogical concepts can be tested empirically. Moreover, they normally are woven into theories which have a mathe-matical expression, presupposing the possibility of measuring quantitatively some aspects of the phenomena under considera-tion. This is not the case in regard to theology. No testing em-pirically, it will be said. No mathematical expression, it will be said. No measurement of the phenomena, it will be said. In other words: analogy is respectable in science, but only because science imposes certain conditions on the interpretation and verification of analogy.

Let us take up the verification issue. Unfortunately statements about electrons concern all electrons, wherever. But we cannot check on all of them. This means the collapse of verificationism. In its place we have the doctrine of falsificationism, as enunciated by Karl Popper, and then bowdlerized by the post-positivists. Falsificationism is the doctrine that the test of whether something is a scientific claim is this: can it be in principle falsified by observation, etc.? Popper used it as a means of distinguishing metaphysics from science, not as a criterion of meaning. But Professor Flew and others have used it in the latter sense. Result: the doctrine that what is unfalsifiable cannot be true, because meaningless; but the analogical talk about radio-waves is all right, because it is experimentally and/or observationally falsifiable. You can always knock down a theory. But this seemingly is not true of theology. How can you falsify (experimentally or observationally) the doctrine of Creation? How could you ever do so?

Such is the argument. The answers are various. For instance, falsificationism has the following sort of Achilles' heel. Suppose you want to falsify a law, you do an experiment. It contradicts the law, let us say. But you are not going to scrap a perfectly good law because it has a seeming exception. You try the experiment again and again. In short, you formulate a micro-law, which infringes the macro-law. In the experimental context, it is the regularity that knocks out the law. In this context, this argument means the partial collapse of falsificationism. For you cannot check on all instances of the micro-law.

Still, falsificationism has much to be said for it, and can hit back. It can hit back by distinguishing between theoretical and inductive laws. An inductive law is where you are bombarded by instances and end up saying 'Whenever this then that' or 'All these are like that'. Such a law has the barest minimum of theoretical content. A theoretical law, on the other hand, is one which incorporates a concept applicable to various inductive laws—a concept which, so to say, serves to unify inductive laws: a concept like *electron* or *gene* which helps to explain various regularities. Falsificationism hits back by saying that theoretical laws, in the experimental context, are falsifiable, because in principle one can produce evidence of contradictory inductive laws. In principle, one can produce counter-regularities.

Still, this aspect of scientific method does not bear much on the case of the doctrine of Creation, for experimental laws have to do with explaining some features of the cosmos by others. More-

47

over, experimental laws are not the only sort. For example, astronomical theories, like Kepler's Law, deal with regularities in the motions of irregular objects, namely the actual planets round our sun. But it is certainly not a feature of astronomical theory that every sun should have seven or nine or whatever number of planets, nor that their courses should be elliptical. Fairly recently Professor Martin Ryle produced some counter-evidence to the so-called Steady State theory. In a way, the latter theory tends to assimilate the observational to the experimental. It is an attempt to see the cosmos as roughly the same wherever and whenever you look at it, provided it is taken in reasonably large doses. This gives astronomy the universal character which we associate with experimental or inductive laws. But it looks as though the cosmos is not that uniform. The Steady State theory is susceptible to observational falsification. This is not of the form 'Whenever I try this experiment I get this result' or even 'Whenever this then that'; but it is of the form 'There are more radio-sources over there than the theory predicts.'

Now in one way, though perhaps only in a limited way, the doctrine of Creation is susceptible in principle to an analogue to such observational falsification. For the doctrine is woven into a scheme of belief which includes reference to the historical and experiential revelation of the Creator. This is brought out in its sharpest form in the opening verses of St. John's Gospel. This means that the scheme is analogous to a theory, and the scheme as a whole is susceptible of counter-evidence. Thus if we could conclusively establish that Jesus never existed, or that reports of prophetic experience were fraudulent, the scheme as a whole would be falsified. Thus the logic of religious claims is not all that diverse from the logic of scientific theories. Thus the objection which was raised against the use of analogies in theology has less substance than appeared at first.

Moreover the personal nature of God means that a closer analogue to the doctrinal scheme which delineates theistic belief is a biographical narrative. But here the possibility of positive evidence is as important as the possibility of falsification.

Still the objection to analogies in theology may go further, and ask how it is that we use, in particular, the analogy of Creation out of nothing. Is this not a concept which has no bearing on the way we talk of making something—pots are made out of clay, are they not?

Here an examination of scientific and artistic creativity is important, for it may help to loosen up our literalistic prejudices. As it happens, scientific creativity also can teach an important lesson about the logic of the religious situation.

Here I come at last to Galileo Galilei. He can serve as an instance of a breakthrough in scientific insight. Allegedly he went up the leaning tower of Pisa to test an aspect of Aristotelianism empirically and experimentally. In fact, he worked out *a priori* that a large weight would hit the ground at the same time as a lesser one, by the thought-experiment of considering what the Aristotelian answer ought to be if we suppose that the two weights are joined. Galileo also, it will be recalled, was deeply attracted by the new Copernican theory. In both cases we detect more than an experimental or observational advance (though it would be wrong to underestimate the importance of the telescope in revealing those wrinkles on the moon and those moons round Jupiter which exploded a whole lot of earlier speculation). Here were instances of scientific advance which owed much to a conceptual revolution. The most marked case, of course, of a conceptual revolution was that achieved by Einstein. I wish therefore to propound the not very original thesis that a major component of scientific advance is the creation of new ways of looking at the phenomena.

These ways are not just the product of inspecting events, though sometimes facts can be suggestive. Nor are they deducible from previous theorizing: they transcend the tradition, though they nevertheless belong to it. They are thus not just a rearrangement of existing elements. Already we can say that they bring into existence something radically novel in the history of ideas. Such radical novelty begins to look like the creation of something from nothing. Or more properly, it is perhaps odd to ask 'Out of what did Galileo or Copernicus or Einstein construct their theories?' If, then, we want the beginnings of a comparison between the doctrine of Creation and something in human experience we can look to artistic and scientific creativity.

But just as important is the lesson we can learn about the nature of knowledge. Here in the creation of new ways of interpreting phenomena—in the conceptual revolutions which have advanced understanding—there is necessarily a leap both beyond previous concepts and beyond the evidence. This is where verificationism can never fully work. It is also why phenomenalism, which tries to interpret assertions about the world in terms of sense-experience, is unable to cope with scientific imagination. It is also the reason why old pictures of induction are inadequate to the character and history of scientific discovery. The attempt to restrict knowledge to conform to narrow empiricist epistemologies of this kind is fatal. This is what makes the present trends in the philosophy of religion so ironic. They involve a kow-tow to doctrines that do not even work in science.

Once we have rid ourselves of these manifestations of empiricism, we can resume boldness in the affirmation of the doctrine of Creation. This, as we have seen, necessarily includes the notion of a transcendent being, continuously sustaining the world, and indeed secretly present to us everywhere. This is the keystone of the theistic theory of Creation, and the keystone of its explanation of the existence and ongoing of the cosmos. It is also the concept which shows us lucidly that the doctrine of Creation is not a bit of pseudo-science, though we must not neglect the service rendered by real science in destroying pseudo-scientific elements in some traditional interpretations of revelation.

A further point should be noted. The doctrine that there is no form of knowledge which goes beyond that which is in principle discoverable by the scientific examination of the cosmos or bits of the cosmos is a philosophical one. It necessarily transcends science, for it is about the limits of science. Consequently, it is part of theology to make the philosophical claim that such

50

scientism is incorrect. There would of course be no motive to do so unless there were something called the self-revelation of God (or some such religious analogue). Thus in this respect philosophizing is necessarily involved in theology.

But we have also seen that scientific and philosophical criticism of theological claims is itself a necessary element in the proper appreciation of revelation. Without it, theism is liable to become anthropomorphic and pseudo-scientific. Thus even if in theory we adopt a revelationist position, like that of Karl Barth, and claim to have nothing to do with human ideas, we are in fact secretly presupposing the results of advances in human knowledge.

In short: religious truth is too important to be left to Biblical Theologians.

But conversely, philosophical inquiry is too important to be left to the philosophers alone.

I conclude that there is an inner logic which implies that theology must always look outwards on to the frontiers of philosophy and science.

CHAPTER III

HISTORY AND THE ENIGMATIC FIGURE OF BARABBAS*

The accounts of the trial and death of Jesus form a substantial part of the Gospels. The accounts are in many ways dramatic and moving. But they also bristle with difficulties. To go into these problems may illustrate the refreshing and exciting difference made to our thinking about the texts by the method of open historical research.

Let me rehearse the difficulties.

The first, and perhaps principal difficulty, is that Pilate asks the crowd whether they wish him to release Jesus or Barabbas. This so-called *privilegium paschale*, according to which the Jews had the choice of a prisoner for release at the time of the Passover is nowhere else attested. Moreover, the choice is represented as a straight one between two candidates. Even supposing the custom did exist—and this is highly doubtful, since the Jews were extremely meticulous in recording legal observances— there were at least two other condemned prisoners awaiting execution, who, you will of course recall, were crucified together with Jesus. Why then should Barabbas be the only alternative to Jesus? To obviate this difficulty it might be supposed that Pilate customarily nominated the candidates, and in this case nominated Jesus and Barabbas. But Barabbas is represented as being an insurrectionary. It is odd that Pilate would have nominated a political terrorist rather than a common criminal. In brief, the whole account of the *privilegium paschale* as it is commonly interpreted is open to doubt.

---

* Since this was written, I have discovered a not dissimilar argument propounded by H. A. Rigg, Jr., in the *Journal of Biblical Literature*, Vol. 64 (1965), pp. 417–56.

A second difficulty surrounds the figure of Pilate. In the Gospel narratives as they stand, he is represented as weak, but fundamentally concerned to do the right thing by the man Jesus brought before him. But our information from Josephus and other sources depicts him as inflexible, cruel, cynical and corrupt. We might explain this by the hypothesis which is commonly advanced by New Testament scholars that the writers were concerned for various reasons to lay the blame on the Jews and to exonerate Roman authority as far as possible. Nevertheless, though there is undoubted substance in this hypothesis, there is, as I shall show, another account which removes the objection.

A third difficulty, or rather nest of difficulties, surrounds the accounts of the proceedings before the Jewish authorities. For the moment, we can concentrate on the chief problem: why was there a difference in the charge or charges for which Jesus was arraigned before the Sanhedrin and the charge under which he was tried before Pilate? In *Mark*, for instance, Jesus was charged before the Sanhedrin for blasphemy; at first, because of disagreement among the witnesses, it looked as though the charge would not stick. But after Jesus admitted that he was the Messiah, Son of the Blessed One, the High Priest obtained a unanimous verdict that he was worthy to die. But then when Jesus was brought before Pilate, Pilate's question is as to whether Jesus admits being king of the Jews. This is not a charge of blasphemy as such.

Let us explore this matter a little further, for the more we go into it the more curious and complicated it becomes. According to Jewish law, the offence of blasphemy required precise reference to the divine name. It is, to say the least, extremely doubtful whether the claim to be Messiah as such would constitute blasphemy. But to claim to be Son of God might indeed so constitute blasphemy, though some scholars have been sceptical as to whether Jesus did in fact use this title at all. And as we shall see, the title would normally have been interpreted in another way. At any rate, we seem to be able to rule out the idea that a claim to be king of the Jews (Messiah in a political sense) would have attracted the legal condemnation of Jesus before the Sanhedrin. Now suppose that the Jewish court indeed made a charge of blasphemy stick, why was Jesus not then condemned to death by stoning, which was the Jewish penalty? Two possibilities emerge: either the Jews were no longer empowered to put people to death, as St. John's Gospel claims; or, though they could in principle have executed Jesus, they could not make the charge of blasphemy stick.

The first possibility is supported by St. John's Gospel: the Jews tell Pilate: 'We are not allowed to put him to death.' That the Jews had at this time no right to inflict the death penalty has been much disputed by scholars, but it is significant (as Professor C. H. Dodd has recently argued) that there is external evidence, from a Jewish source, that criminal jurisdiction was taken away from the Sanhedrin about this time. It is probable therefore that the proceedings before the Sanhedrin were designed to establish Jesus' essential guilt, though a religious charge of blasphemy could scarcely be brought before a Roman court.

Thus we may conclude, on this point, that the real cause for the Jewish hostility to Jesus was his supposed blasphemy, and he therefore, in the eyes of the Sanhedrin, deserved to die; but the way of achieving this task was by arraigning him on a political charge before Pilate.

Nevertheless, a difficulty remains. As was remarked earlier, a charge of blasphemy required precise reference to the divine name: but it is notable in *Mark* that Jesus' reply to the High Priest carefully avoids such a usage. Moreover, Jesus' acknowledgement of Messianic status would not to Caiaphas have meant a claim to divine nature, for the Messiah as son of God was in current Jewish thought conceived as a human figure. Thus we are left with the paradox that the Sanhedrin thought Jesus deserved to die, because of his blasphemy, but yet could not claim that he had committed blasphemy. However, we shall later see a solution to this difficulty.

A fourth main difficulty with the account of Jesus' trial or rather trials is that there are great discrepancies between the account in the Gospels of the hearing before the Sanhedrin and the rules of that court as described in the *Mishnah*. The net result is to suggest that if the Gospels are correct, the Sanhedrin committed various illegalities in the trial. Yet this is odd, since it was not an early Christian charge against the Jews—and in view of the anti-Jewish tendency of some of the scriptural writings, this omission would be perplexing. Two main ways out of this problem have been posed. The first is to say that the relevant tract in the *Mishnah* dates from a much later period (about A.D. 200) and does not describe the rules operative at the time of Jesus. The second way out is to say that Jesus' appearance before the Sanhedrin did not constitute a formal trial, but informal proceedings designed to establish the desirability of bringing Jesus before the Roman court. Against the first solution, it can be replied that nevertheless the temper of the *Mishnah* is conservative in the important sense that the rabbis took great pains to base themselves upon tradition. Hence, though there is no reason to think that the *Mishnah* account of the rules exactly corresponds to the situation at the time of Jesus, it can at least indicate the main structure of criminal jurisdiction at that time. Against the second solution it can be pointed out that a formal verdict was passed on Jesus, judging from the account in *Mark*. And a verdict presupposes a formal trial.

These difficulties have occasioned a third attempted solution —namely that the proceedings were informal, but that Mark wrongly thought them to be formal. This would square with the account in *John*.

However, it may not make much difference whether we treat the proceedings as formal or informal: they were still proceedings which were designed to assure the Sanhedrin that Jesus was guilty of the charge of blasphemy. If indeed the criminal jurisdiction of the Sanhedrin was at this time suspended, and that too recently, it would be natural for the Sanhedrin to treat their own proceedings as equivalent to a kind of Grand Jury to establish whether Jesus should be taken before Pilate. Moreover, the frustration of having someone who deserved by divine law to die but whom they could not execute would make recourse to Pilate's court a logical course to adopt. But all this is predicated on the assumption that the Sanhedrin had genuine grounds for believing Jesus to be a blasphemer. And this brings us back to the third main difficulty in the narrative—that we are quite unclear, given the present accounts, that Jesus was in fact guilty of blasphemy in the legal sense.

Another difficulty with the Gospel narrative is that Jesus was betrayed by Judas. What did this betrayal consist in? What was it that Judas betrayed? According to the narrative, the main function of Judas was to lead the group who were to make the arrest to Jesus. Yet, as Jesus himself pointed out at the time of his arrest, there was no need for them to come at him by night, as though he wese an insurrectionist. For he openly preached and taught during the day-time. If the object was to arrest him without fuss, this implied a strong measure of public support for Jesus. This in turn raises the question of the motive for getting rid of him. This is no doubt not unconnected with the motive on the part of Judas in betraying him. Various possibilities present themselves.

First, suppose Jesus was intending a revolution (despite all the counter-evidence), then it would be necessary to apprehend him with speed. On this interpretation, Judas would betray the secret of the impending revolution. Several objections to this possibility emerge: first, there would be no need for the proceedings against Jesus on the score of blasphemy: second, the likelihood about Judas is the opposite one—that Judas was a Zealot, who looked to a military and political solution to Israel's problems; third, Jesus' prior actions do not support this interpretation.

Second, suppose that the Sanhedrin's real objections to Jesus were religious ones, the authorities need not have acted so much in haste at the last moment before the Passover feast. If in general they were out to get him, as indeed the narratives suggest, they could have got him earlier; and if Jesus was using Gethsemane as a hiding place, which needed the inside information of Judas to reveal, this hardly squares with his public appearances during the day-time.

For these reasons, scholars have proposed hypotheses about the content of Judas' betrayal—that, for instance, he revealed to the authorities the fact that Jesus claimed to be Messiah, or that Jesus said that he could destroy and rebuild the Temple, or that the events of the Last Supper marked the inauguration of the New Kingdom and a transcendence of the Passover, etc. These possibilities are largely speculative, and must be tested by the following criterion: Does the supposed content of Judas' betrayal reveal anything to the Sanhedrin which would make a good basis for a charge of blasphemy? We have seen that the claim to be Messiah was itself insufficient; the same goes for the claim to be able to destroy the Temple and rebuild it; it is doubtful whether the events of the Last Supper by themselves would work either as such a basis. In short, the content of Judas' betrayal would have to be something deeper, to which the claims about Messiah, etc., could point.

Another, but smaller difficulty, about the account of the proceedings before the Sanhedrin is that the witnesses at first failed to agree about their evidence. As the implication is that the witnesses were 'false witnesses', i.e. that they were suborned, this disagreement testifies to a remarkable inefficiency on the part of those who started the affair. A solution to this problem is to suppose that the proceedings were correctly conducted, and that what the witnesses said did not show unambiguously that Jesus was guilty of blasphemy. As we shall see, there may be an explanation of this, in terms of the theory about Barabbas which I shall shortly propound.

There is also a certain enigma about the scene in which Jesus is dressed up as a mock king. In *Mark* he is mocked by the Sanhedrin; in *Luke*, he is mocked by the picket which guarded him, and also dressed in a bright robe by the order of Herod Antipas (to whom, according to this Gospel alone Pontius Pilate referred the case); in *Matthew*, he is mocked by the soldiery, but after sentence had been passed by Pilate; in *John* he is mocked, seemingly, before final sentence—the mockery here leads up to the dramatic scene in which Pilate says: 'Behold the man', *ecce homo*. These discrepancies lead us to suppose that there was some tradition of Jesus' being mocked, though precise memory of the place it took in the proceedings had been lost by the time the Gospels were written up.

But there is a significant parallel which was noticed quite long ago, and formed the basis of a speculative theory about Barabbas advanced by Loisy. Philo records a story of a Jew being dressed up as a mock king in Alexandria, during Agrippa I's visit to the city, shortly after being created King of Judea by Caligula. Further, there was a custom at at least two ancient festivals of dressing up a man as a mock king while another was ritually killed. Usually convicts were selected for these roles. Now the name of the Alexandrian Jew was Karabās, and Loisy speculated that Barabbas was some kind of corruption of this name. Thus 'Barabbas' stands for a mock king. Because of later confusion, on this theory, Barabbas was treated in the Gospels as a real person, when he was only a name for the role which Jesus played during the mockery.

The parallels are suggestive, but Loisy's theory fails to explain the really rather great transition from *Karabās* to *Barabbas*, and thus is scarcely plausible. Nevertheless, we may gain some insight into the mockery through the parallels: we may still retain the core of the point being made—namely that Jesus was treated as mock king while someone else was to be ritually slaughtered. But then we meet the paradox that it was Jesus himself who was killed. We shall see that there is a solution to this problem.

There are other difficulties about the trial and death of Jesus, but these seem to be the principal ones. Let us rehearse them again briefly. There is the difficulty of the *privilegium paschale*: I shall call this the 'release problem'. There is the difficulty about Pilate's character: I shall call this the 'Pilate problem'. There is the difficulty about the status of the proceedings before the Sanhedrin: I shall refer to this as the 'Sanhedrin problem'. There is the difficulty about what it was that constituted Jesus' blasphemy: I shall refer to this as the 'blasphemy problem'. There is the difficulty about what Judas betrayed: I shall refer to this as the 'Judas problem'. There is the difficulty about the disagreement of the witnesses: I shall refer to this as the 'witness problem'. Finally there is the question of the significance of the mockery: I shall refer to this as the 'mockery problem'.

The hypothesis which I am about to advance will make sense of these problems; but before I bring it forward, let us observe some strange straws in the wind. As C.S.C. Williams wrote in 1951: 'It is generally agreed today that there is good evidence for Barabbas' full name being Jesus Barabbas'.* Some manuscripts have the name 'Jesus' before 'Barabbas' in *Matthew* xxvii, 16 and 17. For various reasons this is almost certainly the original reading, and the New English Bible uses it: 'There was then in custody a man of some notoriety, called Jesus Bar-Abbas. When they were assembled Pilate said to them, "Which would you like me to release—Jesus Bar-Abbas, or Jesus called Messiah?" ' There can be little doubt that the first name of Barabbas was omitted because of the sanctity which Christ's name acquired.

Another straw in the wind is this: in two of the Gospels— *Luke* and *John*—the explanation of who Barabbas was has the character, one suspects, of a gloss. Thus *Luke* xxiii, 19 reads: ' "Give us Barabbas." (This man had been put in prison for a rising that had taken place in the city, and for murder.)' That this is gloss-like is further indicated by the fact that an extra gloss 'At festival time he was obliged to release one person for them' is added in some manuscripts after the above words. Again *John* xix, 40 reads: '. . . "We want Barabbas!" (Barabbas was a bandit.)' What of the other two Gospels? Here again there is some indication that the explanatory remarks about the custom of releasing a prisoner and the detention of Barabbas is an interpolation.

The phraseology of *Mark*'s Greek is strange, and it is almost

* *Alterations to the Text of the Synoptic Gospels and Acts*, Oxford, 1951, p. 31.

certain that here too the name 'Jesus' before 'the one called Barabbas' has dropped out. Thus *Mark* may have read : 'At that time Jesus, the one known as Barabbas, was then in custody.' But if so the rest of the passage does not read well. The first use of the name Jesus thereafter comes two or three sentences later : 'For he knew it was out of spite that they had brought Jesus before him.' But which Jesus, we ask? And then : 'But the chief priests incited the crowd to ask him to release Jesus rather than Barabbas.' These sentences would not follow naturally from the original text. Consequently we may infer that the explanation of the *privilegium paschale* and of the identity of Barabbas have been interpolated. If this is true of *Mark* it will hold for the very similar account in *Matthew*.

From all this we can infer that the original material reproduced Pilate's question as to whether he should release Jesus or Barabbas, and that various annotations of this question have been worked into the text. Since the annotations (to quote Paul Winter's words) 'supply no trustworthy information concerning the cause of Barabbas' imprisonment, and none of its duration',[*] we can perhaps begin to look at the question of the identity of Barabbas without the preconceived ideas that a simple reading of the Gospels might suggest.

My next straw in the wind is more intriguing. We note that in *Mark*, for instance, we have ὁ λεγόμενος βαραββᾶς : 'the one who is called Barabbas'. As Professor D. E. Nineham remarks, 'if the name *Jesus* once preceded it . . . the meaning would have been "Jesus, surnamed Barabbas" ',[†] and he goes on to cite similar uses of the expression λεγόμενος in *Matthew*. It is most interesting that in all these cases which he refers to the phrase comes before not a surname or patronymic, but a title or nickname : in i, 16, Christ ; in iv, 18, Peter ('the Rock') ; in x, 2 the same ; in xxvii, 17, Barabbas and Christ ; in xxvii, 22, Christ. In brief, we are probably dealing here with a nickname or title. From this perspective, the meaning of the term *Barabbas* is important. It

* *The Trial of Jesus*, Berlin, 1961, p. 97.
† *Saint Mark*, London, 1963, p. 416.

means, of course, 'Son of the Father', 'Son of Abba'. And if there is one thing characteristic of Jesus' own piety it was his unusual use (unique use) of this affectionate term 'Abba' in addressing God—a term used by a child of his human father.

Let us bundle up these straws in the wind. First, Barabbas was called Jesus. Second, the accounts of him are essentially glosses. Third, Barabbas was a nickname or title. Fourth, it means 'Son of Abba'. Fifth, it was a unique feature of Jesus' religion to use 'Abba' in addressing God.

The conclusion is simple, striking and fruitful.

The conclusion is that 'Barabbas' was Jesus' own nickname. Given this hypothesis, many of the problems are open to solution. And, moreover, some new light is thrown on Jesus' own claims about himself.

Let us consider the sea-change which this interpretation brings about in the understanding of the accounts of the trial of Jesus before Pilate. Perhaps it is easiest to bring this out by reference to *Matthew*, with a little commentary of my own interpolated.

'Jesus was brought before the Governor; and as he stood there the Governor asked him, "Are you the king of the Jews?" ' That is to say, Pilate was asking whether Jesus was the Anointed One or Messiah or Christ—these terms being understood in a largely political sense. ' "The words are yours", said Jesus'— but it should be noted that an alternative translation of Jesus' words is possible: the New English Bible offers 'It is as you say.' The point is that he uses the words σὺ λέγεις, literally 'You say.' I shall revert to this point in a moment. 'And to the charges laid against him by the chief priests and elders he made no reply. Then Pilate said to him, ' "Do you not hear all this evidence that is brought against you?"; but he still refused to answer one word, to the Governor's great astonishment. . . . When they were assembled Pilate said to them, "Which would you like me to release to you—Jesus Barabbas, or Jesus called Messiah?" '

On the present hypothesis, this pregnant question means: 'Would you like me to release the Jesus who is titled Son of Abba or the Jesus who is titled Messiah?' (or King of the Jews).

To put it crudely, the question means: 'Shall I release the blasphemous Jesus or the political Jesus?' And if he releases the blasphemer, this is of no account, for his jurisdiction is essentially over the alleged political offender.

Let us turn now to *Mark*. 'Pilate asked him, "Are you the king of the Jews?" ' That is to say, Pilate was asking him if he were the Christ or Messiah. 'He replied. "The words are yours." ' Once again we have the same phrase, to which I shall return. 'And the chief priests brought many charges against him. Pilate questioned him again: "Have you nothing to say in your defence? You see how many charges are brought against you." But to Pilate's astonishment, Jesus made no further reply.'

Once again, it seems, Jesus refused to answer before Pilate any charges of blasphemy. But he *did* answer, in some degree at least, on the political question. This looks like an expression of 'Render unto Caesar. . . .' Pilate's jurisdiction was over the political sphere, not over the religious. We continue.

'When the crowd appeared . . . Pilate replied, "Do you wish me to release for you the king of the Jews?" . . . But the chief priests persuaded the crowd to ask him to release Barabbas rather than Jesus.' That is, they asked Pilate to release Jesus *qua* blasphemer, whom they could not execute in any case, rather than Jesus *qua* political offender, who could be sentenced to death (or perhaps was already sentenced to death) by Pilate. 'Pilate spoke to them again: "Then what shall I do with the man whom you call king of the Jews?" ' Again, the verb is λέγειν which here may mean 'entitle'. 'They shouted back, "Crucify him!" "Why, what harm has he done?" Pilate asked. They shouted all the louder, "Crucify him!" So Pilate . . . released Barabbas to them; and he had Jesus flogged and handed him over to be crucified.'

I have mentioned above the enigmatic answer of Jesus to Pilate. If the interpretation of λεγόμενος which I offered before is correct, Jesus' words may mean: 'That is how you entitle me.' Or, in other words: 'It is *qua* political offender that you choose to treat me.'

There are details in the other two accounts which it would be profitable to explore, but let us proceed forthwith to consider how the present hypothesis resolves the various problems listed earlier.

First, the release problem. This is resolved swiftly. The choice was between Barabbas and Christ, and only these two, because the choice was over which type of charge (religious or political) the man Jesus should be kept in custody. If Pilate released him on the political charge, he would escape execution; but if he released him on the religious charge, he would die. Further, there is no need to appeal to any *privilegium paschale*. But even if it did exist, which is doubtful, the present hypothesis gives an ironical twist to Pilate's exercise of this duty.

Second, the Pilate problem. On the present hypothesis, Pilate acted in a highly cynical manner, and there was no change of mind, and thus weakness, on his part. Indeed, the cynicism may run deeper, for he offered to scourge Jesus and let him free. Scourging, incidentally, was a pretty barbarous punishment, and sometimes killed its victims. If Pilate offered to let him free *qua* religious offender, then he was throwing in a punishment extra to that of crucifixion. In fact, Jesus was both scourged and crucified. In any event, on the present hypothesis, Pilate emerges as cynical and callous.

But why should he connive with the Sanhedrin to do away with Jesus? The possibilities are these. First, he may genuinely have feared an insurrection under Jesus. But this, as we have seen, is unlikely, for Jesus essentially repudiated a Zealot role. Second, he may have thought that the populace would so adamantly turn against him if he did not dispose of Jesus (and on one or two other occasions he had had to accept the situation in the face of popular resistance) that he would be best advised to deal with Jesus. This does not seem altogether plausible, since it was primarily the Sanhedrin who were keen to get rid of Jesus and they would not have apprehended him swiftly by night if they really thought that he was widely hated. It seems more likely that Pilate was content to play ball with the Sadducees, who had an interest in good relations with the imperial power, in return for an explicit repudiation of political ambitions. Thus in *John* we hear: 'We have no king but Caesar.' In any event, the present hypothesis certainly implies that Pilate was cynical. He may have washed his hands of Jesus, the innocent (from his point of view) blasphemer, but not of the political Christ.

Third, the Sanhedrin problem. On the present hypothesis, the Sanhedrin were essentially and perhaps formally concerned to establish Jesus' guilt under Jewish law. This having been established, the next move was to ensure his legal execution by bringing him before Pilate on a political charge. The substance of the present contention is that the Sanhedrin considered that, for religious reasons, Jesus deserved to die.

Fourth, the blasphemy problem. On the present hypothesis, the difficulty was over the difference between the letter and the spirit of the law about blasphemy. The testimony of the witnesses about the destruction of the Temple and the like pointed to something. As to any Messianic claim, this was used in a political sense by the Sanhedrin. But if Jesus were shown to have used the title or nickname 'Barabbas' and to have addressed God as 'Abba', this could substantially indicate that he claimed to be Son of God in some very special and intimate sense. Since, however, 'Abba' was not used as the divine name in the Jewish tradition, but was peculiar to Jesus himself, there were technical difficulties in establishing the charge of blasphemy, even if it was clear that Jesus was in spirit a blasphemer, from the orthodox point of view. Hence the difficulty in making the charge stick, or rather the indications that there was such a difficulty. In *Mark*, it may be remembered, we have the curious question put by the High Priest: 'Are you the Messiah, the Son of the Blessed One?' Here a circumlocution is used to avoid the name of God. Perhaps Jesus confessed to his title of Son of the Father, but in terms which did not lend themselves to the usual language.

On the notion that Barabbas is a nickname or title, a few words are here in order. It is to be noted that Jesus went out of his way to give Simon the nickname Kephas or Peter and James and John the sons of Zebedee he dubbed by the mysterious and little understood epithet 'Sons of Thunder' or 'Boanerges'. These three held a special place in his circle, as the Gospels make clear. It is not at all fanciful to suppose that Jesus himself had a nickname or title within this inner circle.

Fifth, there is the Judas problem: what did he betray? It may have been just the hiding place. Or it may have been something far deeper, namely the secret name of Jesus among the four who had titles or nicknames. Or, if you like, it was the fact that Jesus claimed to be Son of the Father.

Sixth, the witness problem has been in substance dealt with under the head of the Sanhedrin problem. The Sanhedrin, as we have argued, were concerned to be formally sure that Jesus deserved to die before committing him to Pilate. The trouble over the testimony of the witnesses may have, as we have seen, arisen from the novel locution which Jesus used of his Father in heaven.

Seventh, there is the problem of the mockery by the soldiers. If Loisy was at all right the mockery indicates that the one mocked was a substitute for the one who really died. On the present hypothesis, the mockery was especially ironic. Though Jesus died, he was mocked as the Christ or political king; but the one who really died was the one whom the Sanhedrin, with the connivance of Pilate, were really out to get—Jesus Barabbas, the religious blasphemer.

There are various other smaller points which the present hypothesis illuminates. When, according to *John*, Pilate brought Jesus, dressed in mock-royal clothes, before the assembled people, he said 'Behold the man'. It is perhaps correct to think that Pilate was emphasizing the words 'the man'. Here was the human (political) offender, dressed up as king. Pilate confessed he had no case against him, but what of the other Jesus, who somehow claimed to be υἱὸς Θεοῦ—son of God—or, from the standpoint of Pilate's culture, a divine being?

Again Pilate's insistence on the wording of the inscription on the cross was perhaps a cynical indication that he appreciated the hold which he had over those who professed to have no other king than Caesar.

Are there strong objections to this whole hypothesis? Well, there are some. Above all, it will be asked how the tradition could have been so wrong in its interpolations about Barabbas. To this I make two replies.

First, it is interesting that Paul Winter should have argued, in the course of a distinguished survey of the evidence about Barabbas, that the strongest evidence for the historical existence of Barabbas is afforded by those manuscripts which retain the name Jesus in front of *Barabbas*. Such a difficult reading, when the sacred name of Jesus was prefixed to a notorious criminal and bandit, indicates, for Winter, that there is historical truth behind the story. In one way I agree: in another not. That the name 'Jesus' is retained is a guarantee of some historical memory. That this ensures the separate existence of a Barabbas is not necessary, and is as well or better explained on the present hypothesis.

Second, in the light of New Testament criticism as a whole one can say that the Gospels are remarkably ambiguous. On the one hand the order and character of events is often scrambled; on the other, we are brought face to face with elements of traditions which in their circumstantial detail must most probably hark back to historical reality. In general, there is no objection to the present hypothesis. But in particular also we can advance the following account of the tradition which makes sense of the facts and which squares with the present hypothesis. It is this: that the bones of the tradition about the trial of Jesus were a dialogue or a series of short dialogues. (Dialogue is elsewhere a notable feature of the Gospels.) From this perspective, we can detect a common pattern in the proceedings before Pilate, with some subtraction in *Luke* and some addition in *John*. The pattern, briefly, is as follows.

i. 'Are you the king of the Jews/Christ?' (a question which presupposes perhaps the charge expressed by the Sanhedrists in *Luke*).

ii. 'The words are yours.'

iii. 'Which would you like me to release to you—Jesus Barabbas or Jesus called King of the Jews/Messiah?' (the full form of the question is implicit in *Luke* and *John*).

iv. 'Barabbas.'

v. 'What then shall I do with Jesus called Messiah?'

vi. 'Crucify (him)' (v. and vi. are implicit in *John*: 'Here is your king' 'Crucify him').

In all of the accounts there is the statement by Pilate 'I find no case for this man to answer' or its equivalent ('Why, what harm has he done?' in *Matthew* and *Mark*). But it appears at different places in relation to the question about Barabbas (iii above). In *John* it comes twice, both before and after. In *Luke* it comes before. In the other two Gospels it comes after.

Now if the statement amounts to a formal acquittal of Jesus *qua* King of the Jews it seems to make nonsense of the question of who should be released. It is better therefore to treat it as coming after the request for the release of Jesus *qua* Barabbas. Pilate is then saying: 'I find no case against this blasphemer; but what shall I do with the so-called King of the Jews?' Answer: 'Crucify him.' This reinforces the cynicism of Pilate's behaviour.

All in all, then, the present hypothesis makes sense of the tangled web of our evidence. It also has an interesting consequence, for it implies a rather special claim by Jesus (or at least by those who intimately knew him) concerning his status. It reinforces the suggestion that Jesus considered himself to be Son of God in a very intimate sense.

Consequently, this interpretation militates against the scepticism to which I referred earlier concerning Jesus' claims about himself. Though Jesus often used the somewhat mysterious expression 'Son of Man' to refer to himself, and seems to have been not altogether happy with the term 'Messiah' as applied to him, the Gospels speak of him frequently as the Son of God. This has often been seen simply as the result of a later growth in

67

the Church's pious reflection upon the Lord Jesus. But it may well also have a real basis in Jesus' own thinking.

Paradoxically, scepticism about one particular aspect of the Gospel narrative (the separate existence of a revolutionary called Barabbas) can reduce scepticism about another aspect.

I have gone into the episode of Barabbas in the present detail because it is necessary to see the historical Jesus in the context of historical studies. The hypothesis which I have advanced could indeed be wrong, though I hope that at least it is interesting. But it is recognizably an hypothesis which is in a proper sense 'historical'. It is impossible ultimately to get away from these historical questions as long as we remain interested in the figure of the historical Jesus. Here let me quote an important passage from a lecture given by Professor D. E. Nineham. He is objecting to the kind of cavalier attitude which shrugs off the question of the historicity of Moses with the epigram 'If Moses had not existed it would be necessary to invent him.' Professor Nineham goes on: '. . . but the question is not one which can be settled by any other method than the patient, detailed examination of historical evidence, in the full realization that subsequent discoveries and developments may compel a complete change of opinion. The point I want to make is that a search for final security in a sphere where imperfectly-attested historical events are involved is foredoomed to failure.'*

It is for this reason that open and clear-thinking historical investigation has been and must always remain an important component in Biblical studies. It is worth remarking that a considerable achievement of the Christian Church in the last hundred years or more is the degree to which it has harboured scholars who have initiated us into precisely this approach to the history of the Biblical period.

The parahistorical truth of Christianity I have argued, does involve some purely historical assertions about Jesus. Among these, I suspect, there must be the claim that Jesus

* Leonard Hodgson and others, *On the authority of the Bible*, London, 1960, p. 93.

thought of himself as having rather a special status. There is some degree of paradox in the supposition that the Son of God had no conception of who he was (the parahistorical claim that Socrates was uniquely Son of God would for this reason scarcely occur to us). Of course, the fact that Jesus claimed something about himself does not entail its parahistorical truth. The claim is seemingly a necessary, but not a sufficient, condition of his actually having the ontological status. It is in this kind of way that purely historical investigations are directly relevant to doctrinal conclusions. The hypothesis which I have advanced about Barabbas is merely one illustration of the relevance of historical inquiries to the truth of religion.

However, it must be remembered that the New Testament is not Thucydides: it is a confessional and proclamatory set of documents, and the Gospels are not intended as biographies. There is, then, a limit to what can be revealed through the type of historical inquiry I have undertaken here. Nevertheless, it is through the ferment produced by historical criticism that some of the most exciting modern reappraisals of the nature of the New Testament and its message have been generated.

CHAPTER IV

THE BUDDHIST AND OTHER PATHS*

Some people have tried to argue from religious experience to the existence of God. There are two objections to this programme.

First, a mere induction from lots of religious experiences would only show that there are lots of religious experiences. As we have argued in regard to science, a theory importantly goes beyond the phenomena. Since the doctrine of God has some analogy to a theory it cannot simply be established by the analogous phenomena, namely religious experiences.

Second, some important traditions in religion do not involve belief in God—for example Theravada Buddhism. Yet Buddhism claims in a very strong sense to be experiential. A key term used in the Pali canon is *ehipassiko*: the teaching is 'come-and-see-ish', that is you know the truth of it existentially, by coming and seeing, by gaining the experiential insight which in part constitutes the attainment of nirvana. Now this places a question-mark against any facile attempt to appraise religious experience as essentially theistic (or even polytheistic) in character. That is, it places a question-mark against the assumption that religious experience necessarily has as its 'object' God or the gods.

By consequence, it is not at all easy to argue from religious experience taken as a whole, and including that of Oriental faiths, to belief in a personal God. This is not to say that such experience is not of God: that remains an open question. But

* The argument in this chapter is in part a condensed version of that found in the central chapter of my *Doctrine and Argument in Indian Philosophy*, London, 1964.

our answer will in part depend on the general theological and philosophical position which we adopt and can scarcely be read off from the experiences themselves.

But in addition to this the phenomenon of Buddhism, and indeed of religions in general, places a question-mark at the component of Christian belief which I referred to earlier as the experiential or existential Christ. That is, in so far as Christ is God's self-revelation, he is revelation to us: and this means that he enters into our personal experience. He is in this respect the existential Christ. But the testimony of the Christian here refers to or expresses his own form of religious experience. How do we evaluate it?

We can evaluate it in at least two ways. We can evaluate it as a reason for believing in Christianity; or we can evaluate it as a genuine instance, from within Christianity, of experience of Christ. In short, we can evaluate it externally or internally. I shall attempt to show that from both points of view it is relevant to cite evidence from other traditions. This in turn implies that the comparative study of religion is a necessary part of historical religious studies and of parahistorical religious studies; and in addition it is a necessary basis for parahistory whether this be approached from the Christian, Buddhist or other (including atheist) points of view.

It is perhaps worth saying a few words on the main structure of Theravadin belief, since this has in the past been much misunderstood in the West.

The Four Noble Truths enunciated by the Buddha take the form of a diagnosis of the condition of living beings and a prescription about the cure of this condition. They assert that the condition of living beings is essentially one of dissatisfaction, unhappiness, illfare or suffering (these are some of the transslations of the term *dukkha*). The basic root of this suffering is craving—craving whereby we bind ourselves to the realm of impermanent objects and experiences. But it is possible to remove this craving. This is to be achieved by treading the Noble Eightfold Path leading to nirvana. Nirvana involves the attain-

71

ment of serenity and insight, and means that there will be no more rebirth.

It is essential to the Buddha's message that all living beings (save those that attain nirvana) are continually being reborn. But the Buddha differed here from the typical expression of this belief among his contemporaries. The contemporary doctrine of reincarnation included belief in some kind of soul or eternal self which underlies mental and physical processes and which carries over from one birth to another. The Buddha denied this, and explained rebirth in terms of a continuing succession of impermanent states. This fitted in with the more general doctrine that all things, persons, etc., are impermanent, except the state of nirvana. Thus even the gods are impermanent.

Buddhism does not deny belief in the gods, as denizens of the cosmos and thus as part of the fabric of the cosmos; but Buddhism does not hold to belief in a transcendent Creator or personal God lying beyond or behind the cosmos. The reasons for this aspect of Buddhism are at least three. First, the Buddha's doctrines belonged in general type (though his revolutionary recasting of them was brilliantly original) to a group of teachings, such as Jainism, which concentrated essentially on the doctrine of rebirth and the mode of salvation therefore through methods of yoga and asceticism, and which did not regard the cult of gods or of God as important. Second, the Buddha was much disturbed by the existence of suffering and evil. Third, Buddhism did not accept the Vedic scriptures as authoritative—scriptures which were evolving a doctrine of a Supreme Being.

By consequence of all this, there is no suggestion in the Pali canon that the experience of nirvana is the experience of a personal Being. We thus have a type of religious experience which does not fit easily into Christian preconceptions. Yet on the other hand, it is not sufficient to say that there is a characteristically theistic experience and a characteristically Buddhist one, which is different in kind. It is not sufficient to say this (though in one way it is an approximation to the correct analysis of the situation). It is not sufficient for two reasons.

First, the culmination of the Eightfold Path is the practice of meditation, involving a type of contemplative experience to which there are strong analogies in other forms of religion. There are analogies to it in classical Yoga (which in all probability was originally atheistic); there are analogies in Hindu non-dualism or Advaita Vedanta, where the contemplative life can lead to the existential realization of one's essential identity with Brahman, the sole divine Reality; there are analogies to it in the contemplative life of the Muslim Sufis, and in Jewish and Christian mysticism. In brief, Theravada Buddhism is a religion of mysticism (in the sense of contemplation) but it is mysticism without God (or without belief in God, should I say?). If this thesis is correct, then we need to ask why it is that contemplative experience can take such diverse interpretations in differing traditions.

Here the example of Indian religion in general can be of the utmost value, for in roughly the same cultural milieu we can see great diversities of interpretation, and yet we can also detect certain patterns of experience and ritual behaviour which throw light on the situation. India has been a remarkable laboratory of religion, and we can learn lessons from her results. But to appraise these it is necessary to take a survey of the main doctrines which have been evolved there.

I have already mentioned that Buddhism does not accept the validity of the Vedic revelation, and it does not recognize the dominance of the Brahmins in religion. It is thus commonly categorized as *nāstika* or unorthodox. The two main forms of unorthodox religion in the Indian tradition have been Buddhism and Jainism. In addition, anti-religious materialism (which has very ancient roots) was an important unorthodox school.

What is perhaps surprising is that within the orthodox schools —all those which recognize the validity of the one set of scriptures—there is such a range of interpretation. The Samkhya school, which provides the metaphysical background against which the techniques of classical Yoga were operated, is, like Jainism, atheistic. Yoga itself by the medieval period came to

73

graft on to this atheism the doctrine of a personal Lord, who was not, however, conceived either as Creator or as the focus of salvation. The latter still consisted in the liberation of the eternal soul from rebirth, through the practice of yoga, and in the state of liberation the soul is perfectly isolated, even from the God who may have helped towards liberation. Thus so far we have two schools, one atheistic, the other a kind of restricted theism.

But of course the heart of Hindu thought in many ways should be considered to be the schools classified as Vedānta. The most influential of these is that of Shankara, which interprets the relation between the soul and Brahman or divine being as one of identity, and which is monistic in the sense that Brahman is considered to be the sole reality. Thus the world, in so far as it is considered as something different from Brahman, is a grand illusion. Advaita Vedanta, or non-dualistic Vedanta, treats Brahman as a relatively impersonal Absolute; and liberation consists in the realization of one's identity with it—the existential realization of this. But in fact non-dualism also makes room for ordinary attitudes to the world and ordinary knowledge. From this point of view, the point of view of the ordinary worshipper, the world is created by a personal Lord, who is a manifestation of Brahman at a lower level of reality. But from the standpoint of higher truth, this personal God must be transcended—he is, so to say, implicated in the illusoriness of the world he creates. Thus non-dualism involves a two-decker theory of truth.

But Shankara's non-dualism is by no means the only important system within the Vedanta category. I can perhaps single out briefly the systems known as qualified non-dualism and dualism, enunciated respectively by Ramanuja and Madhva. Both of these reject the two-decker theory, and emphasize strongly the personal character of Brahman. Brahman here is clearly *īśvara*—the personal Lord. Thus already in the orthodox Hindu tradition we note that there are atheistic, absolutistic and theistic schools.

But also outside the Hindu tradition, there is absolutism, as well as the atheistic systems of the Theravada and Jainism. For the Greater Vehicle in Buddhism finds its classical expression in the Madhyamika system, which—at least as it was later interpreted—essentially involved the idea of a negatively-described ultimate reality which manifests itself both as the celestial Lord Buddha (or Buddhas) and as the historical Buddha Gautama. The reasons for this transformation of Buddhist doctrine need not for the moment detain us, save that it had some connection with the development of *bhakti* or loving adoration (worship) in Buddhism.

Thus outside the orthodox tradition we find doctrines quite close to those of Shankara—indeed they in fact influenced Shankara—even if the mythological framework in which they were expressed was somewhat different. To revert to my earlier analysis of religion: the doctrinal dimension of the Greater Vehicle, in its classical expression, resembles that of non-dualistic Vedanta, though the respective mythological dimensions are rather different.

Likewise the doctrinal dimension of Jainism—the belief in innumerable eternal souls implicated in the round of rebirth, and the denial of a Creator—has a distinct resemblance in its general form to the metaphysics of Samkhya. I would also like briefly to refer to the system of exegesis known as Mimamsa. This is a curiosity in the history of religions, in that it is ritual or sacramental in its main interests—and yet it does not believe in God as Creator, nor is much concerned with the gods. Yet this system claims to give the essential exegesis of the Veda—the scriptures upon which Hindu orthodoxy depends. Because of its great interest in ritual acts, this school interprets the scriptures as a series of injunctions or imperatives. If the school has a faint analogy, it is with the Christian pragmatism of R. B. Braithwaite: but it has the notable difference that the injunctions which supposedly constitute the Vedic revelation centre more on ritual than on moral conduct. The gods come in merely as words used in the ceremonial. This atheistic ritualism is conventionally supposed to be the prelude to Vedanta, which describes the normative doctrines of Hinduism. But it is, metaphysically, not committed either to the absolutism or to the theism of classical Vedanta. On the contrary, it formally opposes the doctrines of Shankara and Ramanuja and the others.

At this point I should utter a warning: in speaking of systems as atheistic, theistic and so on, I am only viewing them from one point of view. I am viewing them from the point of view of doctrines. Further I am viewing them from the point of view of the main doctrinal foci of Western thought. Unfortunately the terms which I use to categorize doctrinal schemes can be misleading, though they are as yet the only terms available in English. For instance, 'atheism' implies antipathy to religion, in the West. This is not necessarily or commonly so in the context of the Indian tradition. For instance, the Mimamsa is committed to sacrificial religion; Buddhism is committed to the contemplative life (in the religious sense); Jainism is committed to austerity as a mode of obtaining release, but contemplative practices enter into the form of austerity which it inculcates. Again, the Yoga system depends upon the metaphysics provided for it by Samkhya. But it is distinctively religious, for, despite the atheism of Samkhya, Yoga is a main epitome of the contemplative life in the Indian tradition. If mysticism is essentially religious, then Yoga is. One can indeed trace a family resemblance between the contemplative mysticism of Jainism, Yoga, Theravada Buddhism, Greater Vehicle Buddhism, non-dualistic Vedanta and theistic mysticism in Hinduism, Islam and Christianity. In brief, 'atheism' in this context does not imply anti-religion.

Though it may do so: thus Indian materialism was both atheistic and anti-religious. In a way Buddhism was a mean between the doctrines of Jainism or Samkhya and those of the Materialists.

These varied patterns of belief usually strike the Westerner—brought up, roughly speaking, against the background of the Judaeo-Christian tradition—as odd and surprising. For in a certain way Indian religions seem undogmatic—they seem to allow a great variety of belief. This is partly because the concept of a holy community which determines religious truth is not quite applicable to Indian religion. It is thus wrong to bring Western preconceptions to bear on the history of Indian religion. Nevertheless, surprise at the variety of doctrines has one use: for it brings home to us in its stark reality the point that within the orthodox Hindu tradition we have a fantastic divergence of belief despite the fact that the different schools all profess to be interpreting the same texts substantially—namely the Vedic revelation. Perhaps we can begin to appreciate the point now that we live in an age when atheistic versions of Christianity are being proffered (with suitable quotations from the scriptures).

In short, the Indian tradition is highly variegated: and there are strong analogies between some of the orthodox schools and some of the unorthodox, non-Hindu ones. This already suggests that the determinants of belief here were not essentially scriptural, despite appeals to authority and revelation. I can perhaps bring this out by reference to a chart which displays some of the key beliefs of the various systems in their classical form. The chart, I must repeat, concerns rather the doctrinal dimension of the systems in question, not the mythological and traditional values attached to them in the differing religious strands of Indian religious life.

We may note that all the schools represented here believe in rebirth and in release (moksha, nirvana) as the goal of the religious life, with one exception—Materialism. But not all believe in a plurality of eternal selves or souls: the Materialists do not, for obvious reasons, nor do the Buddhist schools. Non-dualistic Vedanta also denies the plurality because of its affirmation of a single Self identical with ultimate reality.

We should also note that where belief in an Absolute occurs together with belief in a personal Lord, the latter is seen as a lower or secondary manifestation of the former. The Tathagata viewed as Lord in the Mahayana, for instance, points to and is grounded in something more fundamental—the *dharmakāya* or 'Truth-Body', which is both the inner essence of Buddhahood and that Void or Emptiness which is the Absolute.

77

CHART ILLUSTRATING SOME KEY BELIEFS AND PRACTICES IN VARIOUS INDIAN SYSTEMS

an X indicates the presence of the doctrine in question, an O its absence or denial

	Madhyamika (Mahayana Buddhism)	Advaita Vedanta	Theistic Vedanta (Ramanuja, Madhva, et al.)	Yoga	Samkhya	Jainism	Theravada Buddhism	Materialism
Absolute	X	X	O	O	O	O	O	O
Lord (īśvara, tathāgata)	X	X	X	X	O	O	O	O
Creator	O	X	X	O	O	O	O	O
reality of world	O	O	X	X	X	X	X	X
phlurality of eternal souls	O	O	X	X	X	X	O	O
a single self	O	X	O	O	O	O	O	O
rebirth	X	X	X	X	X	X	X	O
release	X	X	X	X	X	X	X	O
orthodoxy	O	X	X	X	X	O	O	O
relative importance of (a) yoga and allied contemplative practices and	2	2	1	2	2	2	2	0
(b) worship and bhakti	1	1	2	(1)	0	0	0	0

It may also be observed that belief in a personal Lord does not necessarily entail the belief that that Lord is Creator. I have also entered on the chart two further significant points: first, an indication of the orthodoxy or otherwise of the systems; and second a rough estimate of whether worship or contemplation is primary or only religious activity conducing to release, etc. I shall have more to say about this shortly.

Certain points emerge quite clearly from the chart. First, there is a strong resemblance among the right-hand schools (excluding Materialism), from Yoga through to the Theravada, and this despite their being a mixture of orthodox and unorthodox. The resemblance is indeed greater than the chart itself suggests, for it is almost certain that before the medieval period, Yoga was atheistic. Its later acquisition of belief in a Lord is a consequence of the growth of the practice of meditating upon the Lord as an aid towards liberation. But since this is only in a weak sense worship, I have bracketed the figure in the worship line at the bottom of the chart.

A second thing which emerges from the chart is the quite close resemblance between Non-Dualism and classical Mahayana theology. This resemblance becomes even greater when we remember that the Self is identified with the Absolute and when we note that though there was no doctrine of Creation in this form of Buddhism, the celestial Lord Buddhas were able to bring into being Buddha-fields and thus exercised a limited creativity.

In the chart I have referred to worship and yoga. But certain distinctions ought to be made. Both oscillate between two poles, the pole of formalism and the 'existential' or psychological pole. For example, Jainism emphasizes the practice of austerity, and is not so strongly concerned with inner mystical or contemplative states; while Buddhism plays down austerities and concentrates more on the inward side. Likewise medieval theism emphasizes *bhakti* or the loving adoration of God (also vividly expressed in the *Bhagavadgītā*); while Vedic religion was more formalistic in regard to religion—it assigned sacrificial ritual a central role.

But within these polarities we can still distinguish broadly between worship (divine ritual and loving adoration) and yoga (self-control and inner experience). (There are one or two other points about the chart and the interpretation it enshrines which are explained in the notes.)

We may now propose various hypotheses. First, the typical doctrinal clothing for yoga was atheistic soul-pluralism. Buddhism for various reasons substituted the capacity to attain nirvana for the concept of an eternal self: but Theravada (and doubtless early) Buddhism unmistakably belongs to the soul-pluralistic group, even if it transcended the soul-pluralism. With these atheistic-soul-pluralistic beliefs went a doctrine of rebirth, which is absent from the early Aryan tradition.

But it appears in the classical *Upaniṣads*, as a new doctrine; with it went an increased interest in yogic techniques, and yogic interpretations of worship and sacrifice. This brings us to the second hypothesis.

It is this: that the *Upaniṣads* represent a synthesis between Brahmanical ritualism and soul-pluralistic yoga. This synthesis was achieved by identifying the self with Brahman, and thus destroying the pluralism implicit in the earlier yogic teachings.

Nevertheless, yoga remained a central interest, and was given its classical interpretation, in relation to the Vedic writings, by Shankara. Worship, necessarily, remained—and indeed by Shankara's day had acquired a much stronger existential content in the form of *bhakti*.

If there was a development in this respect from the more formal worship of the earlier period, it was quite natural, though the full causes were complex: it was natural because worship as it becomes 'existential' turns towards *bhakti* and loving faith (we can see something of the same process in Judaism).

But the case of Buddhism was rather different: its essential yoga was not accompanied by formal worship. Nevertheless, there developed a cult of Buddhas which involved intense *bhakti*. This supplementation of the contemplative side of Buddhism had its culmination in absolutistic doctrines, which

80

made room for both yoga and worship, though the latter was kept subordinate. (Yet in Chinese and Japanese Buddhism there was a remarkable transformation in which worship became dominant, in the Pure Land Sect. Here we even have the position stated that salvation is by faith, and that the 'works' constituted by monastic contemplation are useless for salvation. This was a reversal indeed of the Buddha's teachings, so far as we can accurately describe them through the mists of tradition.) But at any rate we have in the classical Mahayana the growth of absolutism—but absolutism which made a place for loving adoration and the doctrinal and mythological objects thereof.

This leads to a third hypothesis: that a blend between yoga and *bhakti*—or in Western terms, between contemplation and worship—leads, where yoga is dominant, to absolutistic doctrines. We see this in the case both of Advaita Vedanta and the classical Mahayana. The reasons for this 'law' of religious phenomenology (which could also be in part illustrated by Eckhart and certain trends in Sufism) are complex. But the main point to bear in mind is this. The intensification of worship, together with metaphysical speculation, leads towards the concept of a single Supreme Being as object of worship. On the other hand, there can in principle be many objects of contemplation (or if you like subjects—for the subject-object relation tends to disappear), such as eternal selves in a state of liberation; or nirvana, which is not, in the Theravada, treated as a unitary substance, but rather as an attainable state. But in combining yoga with worship, there is a need to postulate a unitary object of both types of experience. In so far as yoga remains dominant, that object will be treated as a somewhat impersonal Reality, rather than as a personal Lord: it will, that is, be treated absolutistically—but room is made for the Lord at a lower level of reality or truth.

But conversely, if worship is dominant, we have theism: and the yogic experience tends to be treated as union with a personal Lord. Since, however, worship demands a sense of the difference between the Lord and the worshipper or worshipper's soul,

F 81

theism keeps off doctrines of the identity between the soul and God. Union is rather a communion between the contemplative and his God, not a merging into the divine essence.

The hypotheses which I have advanced no doubt need refinement. But they constitute a way in which we can make sense of the varieties of Indian doctrine in terms of the different emphases placed upon two sorts of ritual and experience. Actually, the theory can be extended much wider—and can be used to categorize the various main forms of religion. To that I shall turn briefly. The attraction of the theory lies partly in the following considerations.

There are those who think that all religious experience is basically the same. They count Muhammad and Jeremiah as mystics. But if so, why is theistic Islam so very different from Buddhism? The Buddha did not preach a religion of worship and obedience to God. On the other hand, there are those who treat theistic contemplation as essentially different from non-theistic. This means having at least three categories of religious experience—prophetic or devotional; theistic mysticism; and non-theistic mysticism. One could indeed go on multiplying sorts if one believes that the interpretation or doctrinal description of religious experience arises directly and simply out of the experiences in question. Such an idea, however, is unsatisfactory for two reasons: first, it can have no explanatory power; second, it represents a somewhat naïve idea of religious concepts.

It has no explanatory power, for it merely correlates idiosyncratic doctrines with idiosyncratic experiences. It is naïve, because when a person claims to see God or to have attained nirvana, he is explicitly bringing in complex concepts whose epistemological roots lie at least partly elsewhere. Thus, for instance, the doctrine that God has created the world is already contained in the concept of God as used by a theist. But it is hard to see how a non-discursive mystical experience can itself reveal the history of God's creativity. Likewise an experience of Christ presupposes some kind of concrete historical reference to Jesus, and history is not studied by contemplation.

Thus, in order to get a good theory we ought to suppose (what is already obvious from the history of religions) that there is more than one major type of religious experience. But the less there are, given that condition, the more hopeful the theory is. And two is the least number above one. But of course, these methodological considerations must yield to the facts. I also believe that the theory I am propounding covers the main substance of Indian religion, and much else besides—though there may well be a case for adding one or two other types of religious experience in a complete phenomenology.

I could perhaps indicate the wider scope of the theory by asserting the following theses, some of which repeat those formulated earlier in relation specifically to the Indian tradition.

First, where we have strong prophetic or devotional experience, in the context of worship, we have theism—as in ancient Judaism, and early Islam.

Second, where worship of the above character is blended with contemplative religion, but remains dominant, we get theism again, for theism can incorporate contemplative experience. But the stronger the contemplative aspect, the greater the likelihood of monistic or absolutistic doctrines—as in some phases of Sufism and as is suggested in some of Eckhart's writings.

Third, where worship and devotion are important, but are subservient to contemplation, we get absolutism—as in the Mahayana and in Shankara.

Fourth, where worship is unimportant or absent, we get pluralistic atheism—as in Jainism; or an analogue to it—as in Theravada Buddhism.

This is, then, a simplified chemistry of religious experience. It might be objected that contemplative mysticism is essentially the same everywhere and that what differentiates one expression of it from another is the doctrinal prejudices or presuppositions of the people involved. But how could St. Teresa be so self-deceptive as to read a personal God into her experiences? Is not my theory too artificial, too phenomenologically implausible?

But I do not say anything about self-deception. The true interpretation of religious experience still has to be determined. I am not saying that St. Teresa was wrong to see her experiences in the way she did. Indeed, part of my thesis is that the question of the correct interpretation is a parahistorical one which involves doctrinal assumptions and arguments. Thus the question of validity has to be settled in a wider context.

Nor am I denying that the general context may make a difference to the flavour of a contemplative experience. Since Christian yoga occurs in the context of worship and adoration of a personal Lord, undoubtedly there is, so to say, a change in flavour. Since some mystics have used bibulous analogies, let me try one out here.

There is the lemon-juice experience, which you get from drinking lemon-juice. There is also the martini experience. Let the latter stand for the contemplative experience and let lemon-juice stand for the prophetic or devotional experience characteristic of the most intense moments in context of the worship of a Lord. Then the theistic mystical experience corresponds roughly to what happens when you put a slice of lemon into your martini. For all I know the fullest inner awareness of ultimate reality is like martini and lemon; it may be that agnostic or atheistic contemplatives are blind to lemons. Or it may be that only alcohol need be taken seriously. But these questions cannot be settled by simple appeal to experience. For the moment I am concerned with a historical analysis (rather than a parahistorical argument).

Of course, one is presented with a difficulty here. For the attempt to evolve a phenomenology of religion is a bit like literary criticism. There is room for lots of disagreements about the nuances of the reports given by mystics and prophets, in regard to their experiences. By consequence, the literature about mysticism is full of different accounts and approaches. It is also full of indecision on the correct definition of the slippery word 'mystical'. It is also replete with assumptions, often of a theological character, which are liable to lead to bias. There are many axes to grind here. But all this in turn implies something important: namely that some doctrinal or other parahistorical conclusions do look more plausible given that the facts are of a certain nature. For instance, it is easier to defend theism in terms of religious experience if a fairly sharp distinction is made between theistic and non-theistic mysticism, for it then becomes less necessary to worry about the strong interpretative element which, at least on my thoery, goes into the reports of theistic mystics. (Or better, goes into the experiences of theistic mystics.) But if something of a parahistorical nature turns on conclusions we may draw in the comparative study of religion, it follows that the logic of theological discussion itself impels us to the study of religions. But the converse is not true, for the study of religions is historical in character, and does not entail any need to go into questions of truth or validity in relation to the doctrinal and mythological dimensions, etc., of religion.

Nevertheless, it is worth noting here that a certain disease can strike the descriptive study of religion. The disease consists in neglecting or distorting the ideological side of religion—its doctrines, mythology, ethics—owing to a distaste for parahistorical theology. Thus it happens that there is a division in most universities between the sociology of religion and theology. The consequence can be that descriptive studies fail to take sufficient account of the history of ideas. It is remarkable, for instance, how little work has been done, in English, in comparative theology—that is the analysis and comparison of the various manifestations of the doctrinal dimension of religion. To this extent, then, there may be an advantage in a close association between the comparative study of religion and theology. But let us return to the main argument. I have attempted to show that we explain certain patterns in Indian theology by reference to different types of religious experience and behaviour. Nevertheless, this is far from being a complete explanation, since some of the elements in the tradition are of the greatest antiquity—such as the constellation of ideas represented by the doctrines of rebirth and soul-pluralism. They may have acquired their original shape before they became vehicles for contemplative religion. This we cannot know. Nevertheless, we can go some way towards understanding the intimate relation, in the Indian tradition, between the doctrinal dimension of religion on the one hand and the ritual and experiential dimensions on the other. And, as we have seen, the explanation has some relevance to religions outside India.

A consequence of the explanation is that we would probably, at the parahistorical level, be suspicious of a simple attempt to infer from prophetic or mystical experiences to the truth of doctrines. For the explanation implies that different doctrines correspond to different emphases placed upon one type of experience and of its associated behaviour and another. To put it crudely: the Theravadin Buddhist may not be much impressed by prophecy in the Old Testament, nor the Jew by the Buddha's Enlightenment. We need therefore to take a broader view of religion if we are to be clear about the issues involved in the varying evaluations.

There is another important point to be made in this connection. Given that a religious person interprets his experience by reference to certain key concepts such as *God* or *nirvana*, which have wide doctrinal ramifications about the nature of the world, etc., there will inevitably be a gap between the appeal to experience in this sense and the doctrinal conclusions it may be called upon to support. There is an analogy to the problem of induction to which I referred earlier, in the second chapter. For we cannot conclusively verify theories through observation and experiment.

Thus personal testimony in religion, though very important to the life of the religious community, is more like a signal manifestation of the force of a faith than a proof of its truth.

Thus from the point of view of the epistemology of religion, the examination of other traditions has a refreshing effect, in liberating us from the crude belief that personal experience guarantees the truth of such doctrines as we may choose to hang on to it (epistemological protestantism, we might call this belief).

But the analysis of religious experience also poses other questions from the theological point of view.

We may set these problems against the following background. By and large (and thus speaking crudely) those who stress most intensely the devotional type of experience tend to be the most sensitive to doctrinal criticisms. They tend to hold a revelationist position. This is not only true, at least roughly, within Christendom, but can be established (also roughly) elsewhere. For in-instance, Islam is normally fundamentalist about the Koran. Again, Ramanuja, the medieval Hindu theologian who probably did most to express doctrinally the *bhakti* religion, produced a most subtle critique of the Teleological Argument—thus anticipating, and in certain particulars going beyond, the criticisms levelled at it by the eighteenth-century westerner, David Hume. This criticism expressed Ramanuja's conviction that truth about God came from revelation alone.

On the other hand, contemplatives have a certain tendency towards doctrinal tolerance. Perhaps the most typical form of this is the present version of Vedanta, as expounded by Radhakrishnan, the late Aldous Huxley, Guénon and others: this doctrine implies that there is a single truth lying behind all the great religions. But apart from this, religious orthodoxy has had some trouble with contemplatives. The directness of their inner vision has tended to make them see the inward rather than the outward in religion. Thus Shankara himself was heavily criticized by Brahminical orthodoxy; Eckhart was in trouble with the Church; al-Hallaj was crucified.

But an examination of religious phenomenology poses questions against both narrowness and broadness. Thus on the one side the evangelical, devotional man in Christianity, who justifies his position by a double appeal to revelation and to his own experience, could do well to ponder the following feature of Indian religion. The followers of Ramanuja split into two groups, holding two different views of the operation of grace. The one group held that salvation was solely due to the Lord's grace; the other that co-operation with God's grace was a necessary condition of salvation. These are echoes of dispute at the time of the Reformation. But they signify an intense interest in the idea of grace. This idea, in turn, was not merely theoretical, but arose from the experience of *bhakti*: God's majesty and love alike suggested that salvation essentially flowed from him; and the experience of conversion reinforced this suggestion. Here we have outside Christianity a correspondence to the evangelical experience of the Christian. This parallel ought to loosen up the attitudes of the *bhakti* Christian. The naïve assumption that the conversion or grace experience validates, and is in detail validated by, the words of Scripture about justification and so forth, clearly needs examining against this background.

On the other hand, the tolerant mystically-oriented person— who tends to go for Advaita Vedanta as an expression of his position—needs to reflect that doctrines are not simply certified by experience. Non-dualistic Vedanta is only one of the systems through which mysticism has been interpreted. The Theravadin Buddhist from one side will not accept the interpretation—and his is the purest type of missionary mystical religion still living—and from the other side the interpretation will not be accepted by the theist, who weights the experience of *bhakti* more heavily. Thus it is naïve to suppose that there is a central core of mystical doctrine—a perennial philosophy. There may be a central core of contemplative experience, but what this shows, in terms of truth about the world, remains to be determined. In brief, the person who lays store by mystical experience needs to have a more hard-headed and realistic attitude to truth. If the evangelical is too detailed, the mystic is too woolly.

Consequently the study of religious experience generates two pieces of advice. To the adherent of *bhakti* it says: Be more broadminded about other faiths; while to the yogi it says: Truth has, among other things, to do with propositions, and some truths exclude others.

All this has to do with the dialogue of religions, a fashionable idea among Christians these days. The interchange between religions depends on two conditions. The first is that the conversers are not so narrowly rigid in their apprehension of religious truth that discussion becomes impossible. The second condition is that everyone is not so tolerant or indifferent that anything goes. It is useless having a conversation in which everyone says the same thing, especially when it is known that in the background or in the heart there are real divergences.

But the dialogue of religions is an exercise in parahistory, rather than history. It is a polycentric presentation of the fruits of doctrine and attitudes to life. As I have tried to indicate in a number of connections, the parahistorical approach to religious truth must bring in the descriptive and historical. This is one of the ways in which the interests of the committed and the uncommitted coincide.

Whether, then, we look at the Christian faith from the inside or the outside, the diversities and resemblances of religious experience must concern us. It is an inevitable consequence of the logic both of theology and of descriptive religious studies that our gaze should not be confined to one tradition. Voyages can, happily, be both stimulating and refreshing.

CHAPTER V

THE APPLICATION OF THE FOREGOING TO THE PRESENT SCHIZOPHRENIA IN RELIGIOUS EDUCATION

The foregoing discussions have been designed to illustrate something of the inner logic of theological and religious studies. This inner logic drives theology outwards. Even if we begin with Christian doctrine and Biblical revelation, we have to move outwards to the wider world of philosophy and history and the comparative study of religion. I have thus tried to argue, through these illustrative arguments, that a narrowly Biblical conception of theology—or indeed any conception which treats theology as a closed system—is inadequate. It offends, so to say, against the logic of theological inquiry.

If the argument has been at all successful, it may help us to solve the problem posed by the schizophrenia in our religious education, to which I referred in the first chapter.

The schizophrenia consists in the twin facts that Christian education is entrenched in our school system (through the 1944 Education Act) and that the typical modern institution of higher education is secular—that is, it is neutralist in regard to religious or ideological commitment. This neutralism is not just something to do with the charters of civic universities and the like. The neutralism is in part a reflection of the plural society in which we live. Ours is a society where only a minority are firmly wedded to orthodox Christian belief and practice. It is one, moreover, where many of those who teach are humanists (this is especially obvious in the predominantly rationalistic atmosphere of universities).

Many intellectuals, then, are inclined to reject religion: they

90

are therefore bound to be sceptical about the rightness of teaching Christian theology in universities, and doubtful about the propriety of religious instruction in schools. It is odd that an open and religiously uncommitted society should yet attempt, in its schools, to purvey some form of faith. It is true, of course, that most parents, for reasons that are not altogether clear, wish that their children should receive religious and moral instruction of some sort. But those who are involved in running schools and teaching are by no means so committed to this enterprise.

The resolution of this tension can be found, as has been hinted, in the results of the previous argument about religious studies. To bring out the way in which this resolution is reached, it is necessary to set these conclusions in a wider context.

I have argued that even from the standpoint of Christian faith and doctrine it is imperative for theological studies to take philosophy and the comparative study of religion seriously. This means that theology cannot simply be dogmatic. It must introduce, even from out of its own substance, the sympathetic appreciation of positions and faiths other than its own. Christian theology, in brief, must be open, not closed. This conclusion can now be seen from another direction.

What is it that the agnostic may find objectionable in the idea of teaching religion on theology in a secular context? The answer is twofold. First, he may be suspicious or confused about what 'teaching' means here. Second, he may fear that religion or theology is being treated in a closed and dogmatic way. He sees no reason why one view of the world should be given such favoured treatment.

The question about teaching is, in brief, this: that it can either mean teaching *that* or teaching *how*. In the first sense it connects with usages like 'the teaching of the Church on this matter is ...' and implies the authoritative laying down of what is to be believed. In the second sense, teaching is much more a matter of getting people to do things, to think about a subject, to appreciate things. The notion that teaching religion belongs to teaching that rather than teaching how is perhaps secretly entrenched in the very phrase 'Religious Instruction', frequently used in schools in connection with religious education. We shall return to this point later.

The suspicion that religious education is somehow likely to be closed, rather than open, is not altogether without justification. Yet, as we have seen, the logic of theology must drive it outwards. But at present we want to look at the problem not from the point of view of Christian theology but from the point of view of the agnostic whose parahistorical judgments about religion differ markedly from those of the Christian.

I have used again here the jargon-word 'parahistorical'. This can remind us that historical, descriptive accounts of religion may not come under the same suspicion as such activities as the parahistorical teaching of doctrine. Indeed, it would be highly irrational and crass of anyone to deny the importance of religion as a matter of fact in human history and culture. It would be absurd to attempt to induct students into the history of European or any other culture without giving them some appreciation of the role which religion has played and does still play. Religion may be misguided, or a particular faith may be misguided: but this in no way implies that it can be neglected. There seems to be no ground at all for by-passing historical and descriptive studies of religion out of a suspicion about certain parahistorical claims made on behalf of Christianity.

Given, then, that historical studies of religion should have their rightful place in the fabric of education, we must ask about their pattern. It is surely unwise to confine attention to ancient history in this matter. The empirical development of Christendom is at least as important to history, art, music, literature and other liberal studies as is the deep investigation of the Bible. Further, there is an obvious need to involve education in the penetration of non-European cultures. One of the reasons for the continuing failure of so many otherwise well-educated Westerners to understand the attitudes of Asians and Africans is the way in which so much of history is presented from the

92

European, even the colonialist, point of view. Thus the descriptive approach to religion has a wide and open significance, and leads at least partly in the same direction as the conclusions flowing from a consideration of the inner logic of Christian theology.

However, there seems to remain an asymmetry between what is required by the logic of Christian theology and what is required by the attitudes of agnosticism. On the one hand, Christian theology is forced outwards into philosophy, comparative study of religion and so on; and thus is necessarily involved in descriptive studies, of a wide range. On the other hand, the agnostic approach only points, so far, to the importance of the descriptive-historical approach, but not to the parahistorical treatment of religious issues. However, this appearance of asymmetry is perhaps superficial. For I wish to argue that there are educational disadvantages in separating out too clearly historical from parahistorical approaches to the subject.

Before embarking on this argument, however, let us note in passing that already the Humanist in practice sees no profound objection to the parahistorical discussion of religion in certain contexts. For instance, it is part of the normal curriculum in a philosophy department in a university to discuss the supposed proofs of the existence of God, and there are a number of other issues in the philosophy of religion which are commonly discussed as part of philosophy. Likewise, it is unavoidable to have some discussion of the truth or otherwise of Marxism in departments of politics. It would be impossible and undesirable to limit such debates, though it is no part of a secular university's task to commend some particular ideology or view about the existence of God.

One of the reasons why it is incorrect to separate out the historical from the parahistorical—the descriptive from the debatable—is seen from an analogous situation in regard to the history of philosophy. Consider the problem of teaching Plato. One is here explicitly concerned with Plato as a philosopher, so that one is involved with Plato as part of the job of

93

doing philosophy. One cannot therefore appreciate the importance of Plato without entering into the arguments which he uses. To enter into those arguments is to engage oneself in a kind of discussion. By raising objections, one raises questions as to why Plato did not think of these objections, or one is pointed onwards to detect implicitly replies that he might have given. By thus arguing with Plato himself one gets to a deeper understanding of what he was saying. It would be rather arid simply to outline the propositions he uttered, as though it was of no importance to him or to us whether what he said was right. The liveliest and best teaching of Plato, then, is that which without distorting history brings the student into dialogue with Plato.

One could make similar remarks over the rest of the range of the history of ideas. What is the history of science unless we see it as the history of *science*? If men have gone wrong, it is important to know this, so that one can diagnose the reasons. It is likewise important in the history of literature to enter into a critical dialogue with the writers one is considering.

Thus it is educationally absurd, and crass from the point of view of a sensitive and sound appreciation of the subject-matter, to divorce the history from the ideas, and thus to rule out parahistorical discussions from descriptive studies. This conclusion applies equally in religion. Consequently, the asymmetry which we thought we detected between the outcome of the logic of Christian theology and the logic of humanist scepticism about religion scarcely exists. From both points of view, religious studies must be open and outward-looking; from both points of view the parahistorical approach should be included.

We shall shortly see how a recognition of this conclusion should help to redress certain balances in religious and allied studies hitherto. Preoccupation with doctrinal issues, Biblical studies and early Church history has meant that from the theological side many important inquiries into religion have been skimped; suspicion on the non-theological side likewise has affected the history, sociology and psychology of religion.

It is now time to return to the other aspect of non-Christian suspicion: the problem of what is meant by *teaching religion.* Undoubtedly, the assumption of many people involved in religious and theological education has been that a main function of theirs has been the transmission of what the Church or Bible teaches. They have looked on their task as a form of authoritative teaching *that.* But the essence of education, I would suggest, is teaching *how.*

Thus teaching history is vastly more than telling people when and how things happened. It should issue in the capacity to do history—to think historically, to judge about historical issues, to understand some of the forces at work in major historical events, etc. The person learning learns how to do something: he learns a skill.

Is then religious education to be an exception: is it to teach people that God was in Christ and so forth, rather than inducting them into some kind of skilful sensitivity? Of course, it cannot be denied that whatever the subject, there is some information that needs to be imparted. But education and learning transcend the informative. Should religious education not likewise do so?

The situation is confused here, however, by the fact that there are at least two ways in which religious education can transcend the informative. It is often remarked that Christian belief is more than believing lots of propositions. Faith is something deeper than Bible knowledge or acknowledgement of doctrines. So one way in which religious education could in theory transcend the informative is by arousing faith—by arousing love of the Being whom Christian religious teaching is about. It could be then that the function of religious education is evangelistic. It is designed, on this view, to impart faith, and information only as instrumental to that aim.

We may call this first view of how religious education should transcend information the evangelizing view. It can generate a fundamental attack on the present pattern of religious education in schools from two opposite points of view. It can lead to an attack on the grounds that the present pattern is no way able to

95

do the work of evangelization: it would be better for the Church to opt out of *this* project. The attack from the other direction is grounded in the thought that if the evangelizing view is what religious education is all about it ought to be stopped. From the agnostic point of view, and even perchance from a reasonable Christian view, it is no part of school education to impart faith, to indoctrinate and the like.

The evangelizing view in any event seems to be incompatible with the demands of a secular, neutralist society. On the other hand, if a majority of people, for whatever reasons, wish their children to be given religious and moral instruction, it seems that then a democratic society is committed to some version of the evangelizing view (though with due safeguards for those with conscientious objections to the kind of religious instruction given).

The other way in which religious education can transcend the informative corresponds more closely to the way, say, history transcends the informative. That is, religious education could be designed to give people the capacity to understand religious phenomena, to discuss sensitively religious claims, to see the interrelations between religion and society and so forth. It would be an induction into such disciplines as the history of religions, the philosophy of religion, doctrinal inquiry and the sociology of religion. This sounds highfalutin, but when reduced to questions about the meaning of worship, the idea of Creation and the history of local churches, the programme sounds less formidable, even at the school level. However, it is not my present task (even if I were competent to do this) to make prescriptions about the educational technology whereby children of various ages might be inducted into various branches of the study of religion. I am only here concerned with the general aims. There is no reason why the aim of history at school should be the same as history as taught (or as it ought to be taught) in universities; and there is no reason likewise to draw a line between the logic of religious studies at one level of age as opposed to another. Or rather, and this is a vitally important point, education should be seen as a unity, so that the general aims are realized, even if the pattern of education and the modes of approach may differ as people get older.

The second way, then, in which religious education can transcend the informative is by being a sensitive induction into religious studies, not with the aim of evangelizing but with the aim of creating certain capacities to understand and think about religion.

It may be objected that in practice religious education will still, even if we adopt the second aim, remain in some sense evangelistic in effect. For if we induct people seriously and sensitively into the Christian heritage, it is, so to say, an invitation to them to become or remain believers. However, here we must distinguish. It is one thing to present a faith sympathetically but openly (that is, by showing an appreciation of the alternatives to it); it is quite another thing to teach people that it is true while remaining silent or prejudiced about alternatives. It is one thing to present an understanding of religion; another to preach.

The fact is that the primary role of the teacher is that of teacher. A Christian or a Humanist is not, as a teacher, a representative of the Church or of the Rationalist Press Association. It is no doubt the Church's job to evangelize; and provided that people are explicit about their being Church members, there is no earthly reason why they should not preach what they conceive to be the Gospel. But just as a Communist Party member would not rightly teach children in such a way that they were deprived of choice and truth, so the Christian or agnostic teacher should be loyal to the primary requirements of education and the primary duty of being a sympathetic teacher. Propaganda is not the aim of teaching, but the production of a ripe capacity to judge the truth of what is propagated. In brief, the role of the teacher is not that of taking advantage of the young.

Still, it will be objected that people respect sincerity. Above all, young people, who have not been infected so much by the insincerities of the world, respect sincerity. How can the committed teacher fail to show commitment? And is this not a kind of 'forcing of views' upon the young?

I do not complain about commitment as such. It is implicit in the argument I have used about the necessity of the parahistorical approach to religious studies, even where the primary concern is the historical, that commitments should be encouraged to express themselves. However, commitment does not by itself, I hope, imply the bad sort of prejudice: it does not involve distortion: it does not involve lack of sympathy for other positions. It is not that crass evangelicalism which wants to find fault in those who do not agree. Real commitment, I suspect, is secure; and as secure, it belongs to the world of dialogue rather than to the sphere of judgment. It is as willing to listen as it is to speak.

The test of one who is teaching reasonably in a society such as ours is openness, not what his commitments are. The Humanist teacher should give some imaginative grasp of religion; just as the Christian teacher should be able to elicit from his pupils an appreciation of the force of Humanism. The Christian should be able to teach Buddhist studies, and to do so without judgmental attitudes. It should in any event be a cause of joy that there is good in others, not a defensive cause of sorrow and fear.

Thus the sympathetic induction of people into a proper and deep understanding of what Christianity is about should not be bracketed simply with the evangelizing aim to which I referred earlier. It is not absolutely incompatible with that aim, however, for the following reason. What counts as indoctrination and the like depends upon a number of criteria, to do with the degree to which a teacher fails to mention alternative beliefs, the tone of voice used, the lack of sympathy for the criticisms levelled at Christianity or Humanism and so on. A dogmatic teacher or lecturer differs from an open one. The non-dogmatic teacher may be tepid; the open one may be fervent. Fervour and indifference are not functions of closedness and openness. Does the student of literature object to enthusiasm for Turgenev? Only if it is so fanatical as to exclude the very possibility of judgments that Turgenev is rather unimportant. In short, one can reject the evangelizing view, allow the possibility of persuasion and yet retain an open policy in regard to religious education. Similar remarks apply if one begins from the question of why children should be influenced to take Humanism seriously. It is not to be supposed that biases run in only one direction.

All this amounts to the argument that religious studies should be governed by their inner logic, whatever the parahistorical premises from which people start. They should also, I believe, be governed by the principle of the essential unity of education. It does not matter if only one sort of introduction to religion and ideological issues is given at one stage, provided that overall the human products of the system are able to stand on their own feet in such matters: which means that they should not be prejudiced by wrong presentations of faith or unfaith, that they should have some grasp of the meaning of religion, that they should see religious history in perspective, that they should be equipped to ponder these things.

It is true, as we have noted, that parents enter in: for parents have responsibility for their young until such time (too late in my opinion) the young are regarded as independent and responsible agents and thinkers. Since parents enter in, and since parents want some sort of induction into Christianity and traditional morals for their children, one must take account of their wishes. Hence the rather heavy emphasis in our schools and colleges and universities on the Christian faith. But the Humanist need not get violent about this, for three reasons. First, the over-evangelical, rather Biblical approach to religious education in this country has been shown to produce or encourage a great amount of atheism. If children are hypersensitive about one thing, it is unfairness; and if they are resistant about anything, it is boredom. The combination of boredom and unfairness in religious education in schools has helped to confirm a number of generations of sceptics and atheists—many of whom remain interested in a starved way in religion, especially in non-Christianity. Thus the Humanist should rejoice in the practical effects of the 1944 Education Act.

Second, the open approach here advocated could induct people into a more rational and profound evaluation of religious and anti-religious issues, and into a deeper awareness of the springs of religion and of atheism. It might make more converts for Christianity, but for the right reasons, perhaps. It might make more converts for non-Christianity, but for good reasons, perhaps.

Third, in a democratic society, people's wishes are important, and it remains true that most people (no doubt often for bad reasons) want religious education of some sort. Let us suppose the tables were turned. Surely it would still remain essential for young people to know about and to make up their mind on religious and ideological history and issues? The pattern would not change all that much. Less Biblical studies? Good, I say. Plenty of descriptive studies of religion? Excellent. An introduction to the reasons for the Humanist rejection of religion, Marxism, etc.? Fine. Platitudinous induction into Humanist ethics, boring accounts of John Stuart Mill? No, thank you. It would be bad education, and would turn out a generation of Christians, neo-Buddhists and the like.

There is, then, no reason why the schizophrenia should not be cured. It is cured, so to say, by self-knowledge. If we look at what we really want in religious studies, whether from a Christian or from some other point of view, there is no profound disagreement—or there need not be. The battle-lines do not correspond to reality.

Unfortunately the battle-lines have done harm. For instance, at university level and elsewhere they have resulted in an over-constricted view of what should be done in the way of theological and religious studies. This is evident in the climate (happily now fast changing) of civic universities—which have incidentally been influenced by an earlier rather classical and ancient-historical approach to theology in Oxbridge. Agnostic suspicions and the desire for Christian respectability have in the

100

past produced a solution or alleged solution to the problem of religious studies in a pluralistic society. It is what may be called the 'historical solution'—for it rests on the attempt to avoid the sensitive parahistorical issues by representing theology as a tough linguistic, historical, scientific pursuit, mainly to do, as it happens, with ancient texts and ancient history. This approach has reflected itself in colleges of education and schools and elsewhere. Its crudest expression is found in the notion that one can content oneself, in relation to religion, with Biblical Studies, as at one or two universities, or Scripture Knowledge, as in some schools. The historical solution, as I have dubbed it, is the result of something like a conspiracy—perhaps one should say a symbiosis—between agnostic suspicion and Christian conservatism. Its effects may be brought out in a parable.

There was a famous seat of learning in a country where alchemy was still rather widely practised. There was pressure to establish a Chair of Alchemy. But the university pundits were against alchemy. They tended to disregard it. Yet the pressure for alchemy was strong. At last the two parties agreed to a compromise: there would be a Chair of the History of Alchemy. No one could seriously object to that. The result ultimately was a flourishing Department of the History of Alchemy, in which few if any folk challenged traditional alchemical theories, or at least most people tried to refurbish them. Most of the students and teachers were rather traditional in approach.

The parable is not absurd. When I went to the University of Birmingham (which has or will have about the best Department of Theology in the country—I have left it), all the theology taught in the Honours degree was to do with events and ideas before the end of the fifth century A.D.—except for a course in Reformation history. No sociology, no philosophy of religion, no comparative study of religion, no modern theology, nothing about Marxism or Humanism, no Barth, no Bonhoeffer, no Existentialist theology, no A. J. Ayer, no discussion of the relation between modern science and religious belief, nothing about the psychology of religion, no modern church history, no Christian ethics—need I go on? The syllabus was inherited from an earlier phase of development. Now things, greatly due to the forward-looking initiatives of Professor Gordon Davies, have changed vastly. All the omissions listed are now operative. But I do not want to criticize the pioneering work of those who established the Department. They did good work. I merely mention this as a concrete case of the historical solution to the problem of religious education. Its weakness is indicated by the fact that it has been necessary to go far beyond this solution. Yet its effects remain entrenched in the system. It is still commonly assumed that theology, and so by analogy school studies of religion, should largely concern a knowledge of Biblical and ancient history.

However, in the case of school syllabuses the trouble has been caused less by the symbiosis between suspicious agnosticism and Christian conservatism than by the failure of Christians to agree on much else than the importance of the Bible. Hence the heavy bias of most agreed syllabuses towards Biblical knowledge. This leads to an ironic situation.

The irony is that the Bible is a set of Church documents. It has its origin and impact in its use among the members of the Christian community. It is not just Thucydides, but a liturgical document. It springs to life among the faithful. It is to be surrounded by worship and sacraments. It lives in the milieu of preaching. It has its spiritual home in the spirit of the faith. But yet it is studied in schools very often in total disregard of its community milieu. It is divorced from worship. It is presented simply as an historical document. I am, as the third chapter I trust shows, far from decrying the importance it has as a document for the historian. The Christian cannot evade the challenges presented by the open use of the historical method on the scriptures. Yet it is hopeless to fling this set of documents, quite out of context, at the young. The Bible can turn to ashes in the mouths of those who are asked to treat it as a chronicle. An incredible one, doubtless. There is always a need to treat religion as a multidimensional object; and the treatment of religious ideas and documents outside this rich context is liable to end in misunderstanding and boredom.

This is not a covert defence of obscurantism. People are free not to believe or respond to Christian or Buddhist ideas. But before there can be response, there should be comprehension. Before rejection, there should be sensitivity. Before agnosticism, there should be sympathy for faith. Before faith, there should be sympathy for unfaith.

In short, the overemphasis upon orthodoxy and Biblical grounding has tended to truncate religious education at all levels. It has resulted in an over-intellectualist approach to religion as though it is a matter of doctrines and Biblical revelation. It has not sufficiently induced in people a rich appreciation of the whole development of Christendom after the early centuries. It has neglected the sociology of religion. It has failed to penetrate deeply into the nature of religious experience. It has left people rather ignorant of the wider world beyond the European tribe. It has left people unable to estimate Marxism or Humanism. It has said little about the role of religion in a contemporary culture. It has given people much of Hebrew history; much of Hellenistic theology. It has grounded people in the Bible. It has done good things; but it has neither obeyed the ordinary dictates of contemporary relevance (not always a good guide, however) nor obeyed the logic of religious studies. It has served inadequately the next world; it has been a betrayal of this world. It has been a result of confused thinking, the conflict of interests, emotional obtuseness.

But if we can thus be critical of the consequences of a rather narrow theological conception of religious studies in schools and elsewhere, we should by the same token be alert to the rationalistic devaluation of religion which also is over-intellectualistic. It is too easy for the agnostic to think that because he does not take religious truth-claims too seriously, therefore religion is unimportant either now or in the past. It is easy to slip into a facile extrapolation from one's own condition. It is fatally easy to think that other times and societies are like our own. Unfortunately the European, but above all the Englishman, is liable to identify civilization with his own cultural condition. It is but a short step for the intellectual Englishman to suppose that because religion is not very overt in England, it is on the way out anyway. Having lost the Empire we demand the future. Rational folk are like us.

This fatal superiority and blindness has educational roots. One of its roots is religious education, which has not yet sufficiently got people to be sympathetic and sensitive to the way other cultures and times think. Great effort, it is true, is put into inducting students and children into the Biblical thought-world. But this good work in taking people from their experience to a realm well beyond their experience can be so easily vitiated by the evangelical exclusivism of much Christianity. Many young people are brought up to think of other religions and cultures as superstitious, irrational, underdeveloped, though doubtless quaint and in need of love and charity. If they reject Christianity as well, they are prone to a rationalist intellectualism which can blind them to the ways in which other men's hearts throb, other societies work.

Since the study of man is in an important sense participatory —for one has to enter into men's intentions, beliefs, myths desires, in order to understand why they act as they do—it is fatal if cultures including our own are described merely externally, without entering into dialogue with them. This is the basis of my earlier argument that even the historical treatment of religion is essentially vivified by a parahistorical dialogue with its ideas. The agnostic can easily inherit a flat view of religion from the devastation caused by European superiority and religious scepticism. The sociology of religion, for example, should not be conducted on rationalist assumptions, for much is then missed. Anthropology is more advanced in this, for participatory inquiry has long been of the essence of its practice. If theological preoccupations have limited religious studies from one direction, agnosticism has done the same from another direction. The study of religious ideas has been truncated and curtailed—for instance by relegating issues about the existence of God to unrealistic, unidimensional discussions within philosophy, or by treating religious studies as a suspect perquisite of those who are confessionally committed to Christianity. In university practice, philosophy is typically divorced from theology; sociology of religion belongs to a different faculty, mostly; the psychology of religion, so far as it exists, has a place in psychiatry. These divorces are symptoms of the underlying unclarities and prejudices which have been generated in regard to the study of religion.

But my argument has been intended to show that these divorces and unclarities and prejudices are out of place. Christian theology must be outward-looking; agnosticism and Humanism must be inward-looking. Whatever one's standpoint, there can be little doubt that a sensitive appreciation of religious and ideological issues is important in education. There is no need for suspicion and compromise if it is but seen that the essential interests of different positions coincide, and that the logic of the situation demands an open treatment of issues of faith and history.

Happily we are living in an age of revolution. There are signs in many universities and colleges of a transition to a more exciting appraisal of the place of religious studies. There is much debate about the need for a new shape to religious education in schools. It is true that the debate largely has to do with means rather than ends. It has to do with the capacities of children to grasp various kinds of concepts at various ages. It is not yet a fully-fledged revolution about aims. Perhaps I can conclude with a set of theses which will sum up the arguments I have been putting forward about aims.

First, religious education must transcend the informative.

Second, it should do so not in the direction of evangelizing, but in the direction of initiation into understanding the meaning of, and into questions about the truth and worth of, religion.

Third, religious studies do not exclude a committed approach, provided that it is open, and so does not artifically restrict understanding and choice.

105

Fourth, religious studies should provide a service in helping people to understand history and other cultures than our own. It can thus play a vital role in breaking the limits of European cultural tribalism.

Fifth, religious studies should emphasize the descriptive, historical side of religion, but need thereby to enter into dialogue with the parahistorical claims of religions and anti-religious outlooks.

In this chapter I have looked at matters in part from the angle of vision of the agnostic or Humanist. This has supplemented the earlier approach, which has been to demonstrate the need for openness even beginning from the presuppositions of Christian theology.

I have also looked at matters chiefly from the point of view of working from theology outwards. It needs emphasizing again, however, that the logic which runs the other way issues in similar conclusions. Thus if one starts with the sociology of religion, one is soon confronted with questions in the sociology of knowledge and about the 'rationality' of religious behaviour. But one cannot estimate this realistically without adopting some kind of philosophical position. This in turn implies a realistic appraisal of the meaning of religious institutions, practices and claims. In regard to the latter, one need to take seriously what religion seriously says: and this is part discoverable in theology, including, for example, contemporary kerygmatic theology (far removed, at first sight and yet illusorily, from the concerns of the philosopher). In brief, there is a chain of logic from the empirical study of religion to the parahistorical. Whichever way one begins one reaches similar consequences.

It is a happy world. The best interests of both Christians and non-Christians are served by the same aims. The best interests of those who learn also are served by them. It is a happy world—but in theology, religious studies and religious education it is by no means yet the best of all possible worlds.

INDEX

Adam, 35, 36
Agrippa I, 58
al-Hallaj, 87
Aquinas, 16
Augustine, 20
Austin, J. L., 34, 42

Barabbas, 8, 29, 52–69
Barth, K., 23, 33, 51
Birdsall, Neville, 8
Braithwaite, R. B., 26, 75
Buber, M., 40
Buddha, the, 16, 17, 26, 71, 72, 75, 81, 86
Bultmann, 22, 27

Caligula, 58
Copernicus, 50
Coulson, John, 11

Davies, J. Gordon, 102
Dodd, C. H., 54

Eckhart, 81, 83
Einstein, 34, 49, 50
Evans, Donald, 42

Flew, A. G. N., 47

Galileo, 49, 50
Guénon, R., 87

Heim, Karl, 40
Herod, 57
Hodgson, Leonard, 68
Hume, David, 87
Huxley, Aldous, 87

Isaiah, 18

James, Lord, 8
James, St., 64
Jenkins, Daniel, 8, 29
Jeremiah, 34, 82
Jesus, 16, 23, 25, 26, 27, 28, 30, 34, 36, 38, 52–69
John XXIII, 13
John, St., 65
Josephus, 53
Judas, 56, 57, 59

Kepler, 48

Loisy, A., 58, 65

Madhva, 75
Mill, John Stuart, 25, 100
Moses, 35
Muhammad, 18, 82

Newman, J. H., 11, 12
Nineham, D. E., 60, 68
Noah, 35

107